MW00620853

ORDERED BY LOVE

Ordered by Love

AN INTRODUCTION to JOHN DUNS SCOTUS

THOMAS M. WARD

Angelico Press

First published in the USA
by Angelico Press 2022

For information, address:
Angelico Press, Ltd.
169 Monitor St.
Brooklyn, NY 11222
www.angelicopress.com

ppr 978-1-62138-881-4
cloth 978-1-62138-882-1
ebook 978-1-62138-883-8

Book and cover design
by Michael Schrauzer

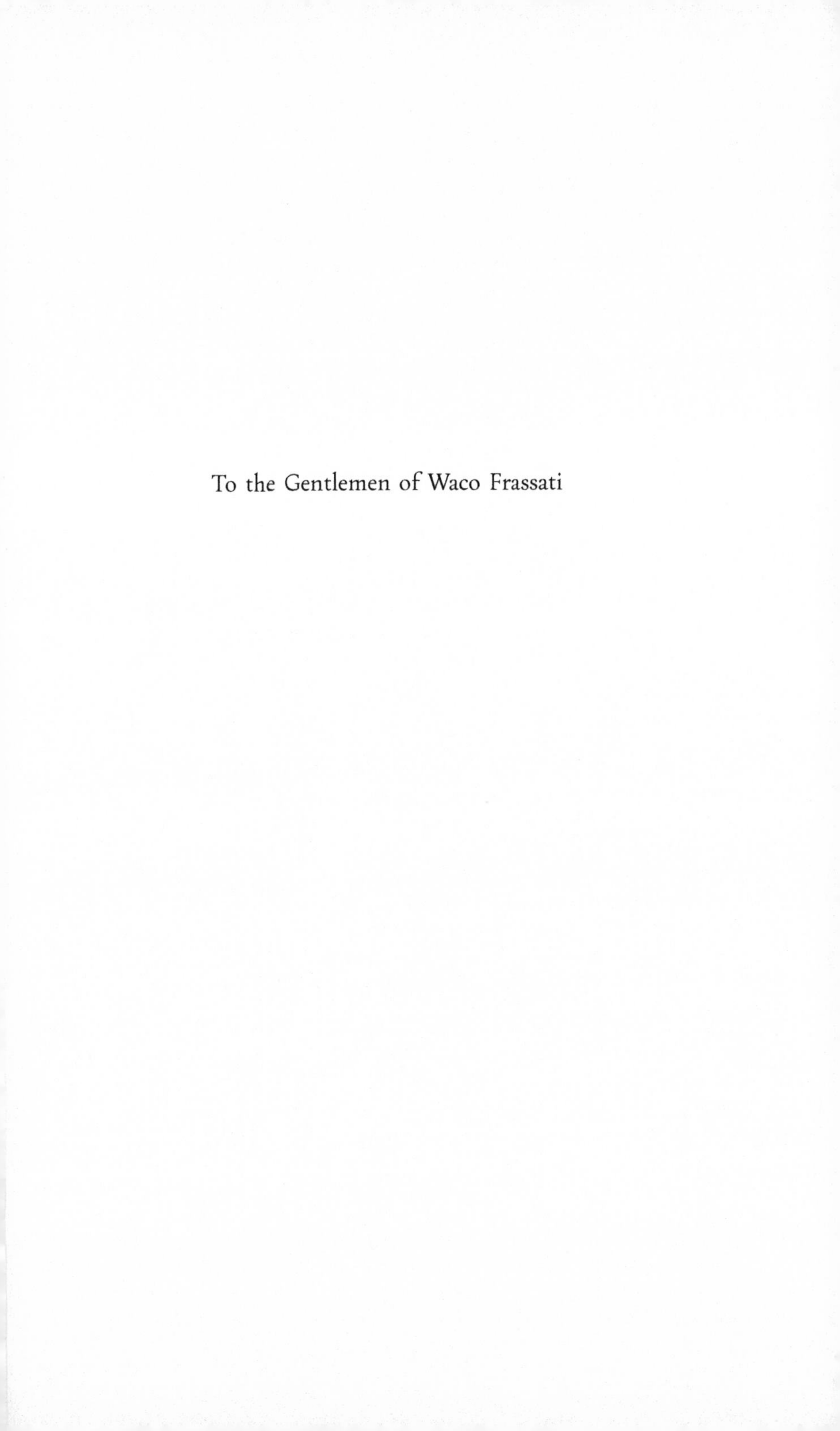

To the Gentlemen of Waco Frassati

TABLE OF CONTENTS

PREFACE

THIS BOOK IS AN INTRODUCTION TO THE thought of John Duns Scotus. It is for all readers with any degree of interest in this enigmatic medieval Franciscan friar. Scholars will find some original scholarship here, if they have eyes to see. But I haven't written it primarily for scholars, or for the sake of originality. I've written it to present to a wider audience the Blessed John I've come to know and love over the last two decades. Instead of an overview of everything he wrote about, I've opted for a narrower focus, the topics curated to present the heart of his philosophical and theological outlook. In lieu of footnotes or a bibliography, I have included an appendix which discusses primary and secondary readings relevant to each chapter. In the same appendix I recommend additional readings to those inspired to deepen their understanding of Scotus.

Chapter 1 makes the case for taking Scotus seriously, situates Scotus in his medieval Scholastic milieu, and offers some speculation about why he is less read and less admired than he should be. Chapter 2 offers a sketch of Scotus's philosophical arguments for God's existence. Chapter 3 discusses Scotus's controversial view about how our words and concepts apply to God, and argues that his view should not be controversial. Chapter 4 offers Scotus's answer to what I call the Biggest Big Question: not *why is there something rather than nothing?* but *why are things such as they are?* His answer focuses on the relationship between God's nature and His radical freedom with respect to any possible creature. Chapter 5 focuses more directly on the created world, discussing Scotus's realism about natures and his distinctive take on Aristotle's idea that material objects are composites of matter and form. Chapter 6 examines the reasoning behind Scotus's most famous philosophical view, that each individual has its own individuating entity: a "thisness" or "haecceity." Chapter 7 is about teleology, or the view that natural things act for the sake of ends; it examines Scotus's understanding of teleology in the light of his emphasis on God's freedom. Chapter 8 considers Scotus's understanding of human freedom, with a special focus on his view that the will has two fundamental affections: an affection for justice and an affection for what is personally advantageous. Chapter 9 considers the virtues that perfect our human nature. And Chapter 10 reflects with Scotus on two perfect human beings, Jesus and Mary. I have written the book as a unified whole, moving from God to creatures and back to God—roughly following Scotus's own order of exposition—but those who prefer to choose their own adventure will discover that each chapter can, more or less, be read independently of the others.

Two questions have guided my writing: what does Scotus think, and why should anyone care? The book was finished when, for every aspect of Scotus's thought I discuss, I felt confident I had given good (or good enough) answers to both questions. By answering the second question to my own satisfaction I fulfilled a personal vow I made shortly after publishing my first, and very academic, book on Scotus. A reviewer of that book, expressing no disagreement with my conclusions, asked in print whether all the painstaking work of interpreting such a difficult thinker as Scotus was worth the effort. I printed out a quotation from his review and taped it above my desk. I determined someday to write a book on Scotus that made it clear why the work really is worth it. Somehow I knew that to pull it off I would need to write as much from the heart as from the mind. This book is the fruit of that labor.

1

APPROACHING SCOTUS

> His language is frequently obscure; a maze of terms, definitions, distinctions, and objections through which it is by no means easy to thread one's way. For these reasons the study of Scotus's works was difficult; when undertaken at all, it was not carried on with the requisite thoroughness. It was hard to find a unified system in them. Not a few unsatisfactory one-sided or even wrong opinions about him were circulated and passed on unchallenged from mouth to mouth and from book to book, growing more erroneous as they went. Nevertheless, there is in Scotus's teaching a rounded-out system.
> —*The Catholic Encyclopedia*

> Yet ah! this air I gather and I release
> He lived on; these weeds and waters, these walls are what
> He haunted who of all men most sways my spirits to peace;
> Of realty the rarest-veinèd unraveller; a not
> Rivalled insight, be rival Italy or Greece;
> Who fired France for Mary without spot.
> —Gerard Manley Hopkins, "Duns Scotus's Oxford"

NEARLY A SAINT

At the Franciscan monastery in Izamal, Yucatán, Mexico, there is a painting of Blessed John Duns Scotus in which he has grown some eagles' wings, wings which associate him with St. John the Evangelist, whose sign is the eagle. After St. John himself, few have peered as deeply into the Logos of God as this other John, from Duns, Scotland, who was born in 1265 and died in 1308. I do not know why Bl. John is not another St. John. For some time in the first half of the twentieth century, things seemed headed in the direction of sainthood. The Scotistic Commission was set up at the Vatican in the hope that he would be canonizable just as soon as authoritative editions of his authentic texts could be produced. But the Commission drags on, and even 1993—about fifty years after the Commission got going, and the year of Scotus's beatification—feels like a long time ago. Yet at his beatification Pope St. John Paul II praised him with great praise, declaring Scotus the Defender of the Immaculate Conception and the Minstrel of the Incarnation. So while I hope there is more honor in store for him from the Church Militant, in the meantime I'm writing this book to help others see something of both the brilliance and the faithfulness of one of the little saints of the little brothers of St. Francis.

Scotus is worth studying, not because he got everything right, but because he got a few important things right, and also because he is a model for Christian intellectuals seeking to put their intellectual labors at God's service. He was ambitious in his efforts, but always deferential to the Church's teaching. He is an heir of that great Christian intellectual tradition according to which truth is unified, whether we arrive at it by reason or by revelation, and all truth is God's truth. And where he thought he could see the way through to a thorough defense, or proof, of any theological or philosophical proposition, he pressed it with unmatched logical rigor, earning the title "realty's rarest-veinèd unraveller" from his nineteenth-century Jesuit admirer the poet Gerard Manley Hopkins; and "Subtle Doctor" from those in his own day.

While he is rightly associated with subtlety of thought and logical rigor, another quality marks what little we know of his life, and that is faithfulness, a faithfulness expressed in both deference and boldness. The deference is evident in his written work at those points at which he defers to the Church's teaching when he comes up against questions to which his portion of rationality gives him no definite answer. For example, he did not think that the immortality of the soul could be proved by philosophy, yet he accepted immortality because the Church teaches it. Again, while he believed in the doctrine of transubstantiation because the Church teaches it, he thought that the purely biblical and philosophical evidence, while consistent with transubstantiation, more strongly supported a different understanding of Eucharistic real presence.

The boldness is evident in two episodes in which his convictions compelled him to take unpopular and possibly dangerous positions on hot-button issues of the day. The first occurred when he was a relative newcomer to the intellectual heart of Christendom, the University of Paris, where he defended what is now the dogma of the Immaculate Conception against the greatest theological minds of the day. That rebellion against theological consensus stemmed in part from his devotion to the Blessed Virgin Mary. There is reason to think that Scotus's support of this doctrine was personally risky: a few short years after he publicly defended it, one John of Pouilly, quoting but not naming Scotus, said darkly that people who endorse the Immaculate Conception should be answered "not with argument but in some other way."

The second episode stemmed from his devotion to the Church: he opposed King Philip IV's efforts to depose Pope Boniface VIII, and was temporarily exiled from Paris as a result. Later he was permitted to return, eventually earning the top Franciscan teaching job at the University. The letter of recommendation which helped him get the job, written by Gonsalvus of Spain, Minister General of the Franciscan Order, spoke of Brother John's "praiseworthy life, outstanding knowledge, and most subtle intelligence," adding that his reputation for these traits had "spread everywhere." But Scotus would enjoy this elite academic perch for no more than two years. For reasons unknown to historians but possibly having to do with those risky theological and political stances, the same Gonsalvus sent Scotus away—for his own safety or for some other reason we just don't know—directing him to take up the far less prestigious post of resident teacher at the Franciscan house of studies in Cologne. The story goes that he left for Cologne on foot as soon as he got the news, not even delaying to finish the discussion in which he was engaged when the messenger came. He died within a year of reaching that gray city, and there he is buried.

SCOTUS'S LEGACY

Scotus's removal from Paris, along with his early death, explains in large part why his written legacy is incomplete and disorderly. There is no book of Scotus's in which, like several of St. Thomas Aquinas's, he says something about nearly everything. His reputation in the early generations after his death rested mainly on two works. The first is his second commentary on Peter Lombard's *Sentences*, begun at Oxford and edited—but never finished—at Paris. For centuries it was known as Scotus's *Oxford Work* (*Opus Oxoniensis*) but now it is known simply as his *Ordinatio*, the carefully edited or "ordered" commentary on the *Sentences*. Lombard's *Sentences* was the standard theology textbook of the day, its prominence owing in part to the magisterial way in which it collated the whole of Christian theology. A master who commented on every section of the *Sentences* would thereby comment on the whole of theology. But in the *Ordinatio* Scotus's coverage is inconsistent: some topics are treated systematically and at length, some very briefly, and a few not at all. Scotus's last *Sentences* commentary, commonly known as the *Paris Reports* (*Reportationes Parisienses*), arguably contains Scotus's most mature thought on the topics it covers, but its coverage is even spottier than that of the *Ordinatio*. The second major work which made his reputation is a collection of disputed questions on a variety of topics, collectively known as the *Quodlibetal Questions* (*Quaestiones quodlibetales*). Quodlibetal disputes were formal academic events at which a master like Scotus would be expected to answer questions from an audience on any topic whatsoever—hence the name *quodlibet*, which literally means *on anything whatsoever*. By the nature of the genre, Scotus's *Quodlibetal Questions* do not represent a systematic whole. History belongs to the organized, we might say: Aquinas's works are today better known and more widely read due largely to the fact that he wrote more, and more comprehensively, than Scotus ever managed to.

Despite this relatively sparse and disorganized literary legacy, Scotus was widely read and honored in many parts of Europe for centuries after his death. Chairs of Scotist thought were established in many universities. Notwithstanding the foundational importance of Alexander of Hales for Franciscan thought, or the resplendent brilliance and political prominence of St. Bonaventure, it was Scotus whom the Franciscans chose as their official theologian, in 1500. This honor ushered in what the great Scotist and Franciscan Allan B. Wolter called the "golden age of Scotism" in the seventeenth century, and in the 1660s the Cistercian John Caramuel observed that the Scotist school was more numerous *than all others combined*. While this seems to have been the apogee of Scotus's reputation and prominence, modern scholarship has shown that Scotus continued to be widely read and highly regarded—at least in Catholic if not Protestant circles—into the nineteenth century.

POPE LEO XIII AND MODERNISM

Then, in 1879 Pope Leo XIII published an encyclical, customarily referred to by its first two words: *Aeterni Patris*. In it, Leo argues for the importance of the study of philosophy in Catholic education; he laments the way in which philosophy, from about the time of Descartes onward, had more and more divorced itself from the wisdom of Divine Revelation; finally, and most famously, he holds up St. Thomas Aquinas as the Catholic philosopher *par excellence*. The praise he heaps on Aquinas is startlingly superlative: so brilliant was Aquinas, Leo teaches, that he managed not only to refute every philosophical objection to the Faith which had arisen before and during his lifetime, but also to anticipate and refute every objection that had arisen since he died!

It is illuminating to imagine what Aquinas would think about all this praise. We can presume he would not be puffed up with pride. Perhaps he would be a little embarrassed. From his life and texts we gather no reason for thinking that he thought of his efforts as the final word on philosophy. And indeed the whole Scholastic method of which he and Duns Scotus were masters was set up to avoid this one-man-says-all attitude. To have the dialectical right to state an opinion, a Scholastic master needed to acknowledge all that was true and wise in the many voices which preceded and surrounded him, carefully distinguishing different shades of meaning and doing his best to resolve disputes between authoritative sources. Always there was the belief in the truth, and the belief that painstaking, charitable reading and thinking could get us to the truth, or at least keep us from falsity. But neither Aquinas nor any other Scholastic I know of ever believed that he alone had finished philosophy—not even the rather hubristic fourteenth-century nominalist William of Ockham.

That particular vanity which allows one to believe he has indeed finished philosophy was not to be pervasively indulged until the slash-and-burn methods of René Descartes and those who did philosophy in his train, especially Immanuel Kant. These and many other modern philosophers took up the unattractive assumption that it had all been wrong before Me and now that I am here I will correct and complete All of Philosophy. This is a peculiarly modern attitude in the sense that it is simultaneously devoted to the notion that there is objective truth to be discovered—a very good devotion—and to the preposterous vanity that one mind can first determine which philosophical problems are worthy of attention and then go on to solve all the worthies definitively. This fashionable hubris persisted into the twentieth century, in the young Ludwig Wittgenstein, whose *Tractatus Logico-Philosophicus*, published in 1921, includes yet another soporific assertion that the problems of philosophy have finally been solved.

Pope Leo XIII saw, and foresaw, the bitter irony in modernism's apotheosis of the solitary philosophical genius: turns out, there were lots of solitary philosophical geniuses, and they all disagreed with each other, about every topic imaginable. The result of modernism, then, must be the diminishment of faith and the rise of skepticism and despair—which is to say, postmodernism. The pope's intention therefore was to muster Catholic intellectuals for a great crusade against modernism and the postmodern monster waiting in its wings, and the crusade was to be fought under the banner of Thomism.

SCHOLASTIC WISDOM

What Leo did not see, it seems, is that by elevating St. Thomas as he did—not too high, but too high above his peers—he risked cutting off Catholic philosophy from the constructive pluralism of the scholastic method with which Aquinas was able to accomplish so much. Imagine if the nineteenth-century Gothic Revival in architecture had revived not the Gothic *style* but one particular Gothic *building*. It is no knock against the Cathedral of Chartres to say that it would have been a bad thing if the Gothic Revival produced only a thousand scaled replicas of it, like a Florentine tourist shop and its thousand copies of *David*. Those who, like me, acknowledge the greatness and overall preeminence of Aquinas but also look to other Scholastics as comparably brilliant and wise take inspiration from

John Paul II's more recent encyclical, *Fides et Ratio*, which promotes "the experience which matured through the Middle Ages, when the importance of a constructive harmony of philosophical and theological learning emerged." While echoing his predecessor's praise of St. Thomas, John Paul II indicated that philosophy would resume its proper role in the life of the Church by embracing a wider array of philosophical voices, and looked to the Middle Ages in general as an exemplary chorus. In this way, *Fides et Ratio* calls us to embrace the best of the whole of medieval scholasticism, and to renew our commitment to the philosophical doctrines that more or less *united* the great Scholastics.

Among these unifying philosophical doctrines are: that there is an objectively real world and we can achieve knowledge of it; that philosophy can demonstrate God's existence; that God is the highest good and full human happiness is conditional on knowing and loving God; that there is such a thing as objective morality and that we can know a lot about it; that the morally upright life is the happiest life; that human beings are reducible neither to chunks of matter careening through spacetime nor to ghostly minds trapped in bodies; that the whole human family shares one human nature; that other animals and plants, and indeed all living things, are more than the sum of their material parts; and that goodness and beauty characterize everything whatsoever, and what we call evil is but the privation of goodness. If every Catholic intellectual believed these doctrines and taught these doctrines to every student at every Catholic educational institution, then we would have the true revival Pope Leo XIII sought.

In this sense Blessed John, along with St. Thomas, is one voice in a chorus of Christian philosophers, one jewel in the crown of Christian wisdom. But unlike Aquinas, he is barely known outside academic theology, and even within theology very few find it worth their effort to read him firsthand. One hundred fifty years ago the poet Gerard Manley Hopkins could lament that Scotus "saw too far, he knew too much; his subtlety overshot his interests; a kind of feud arose between genius and talent, and the ruck of talent in the Schools finding itself, as his age passed by, less and less able to understand him, voted that there was nothing important to understand and so first misquoted and then refuted him." Alas, the problem persists. His own writings, even where modern editors have organized them, are almost always difficult, and there is much that remains untranslated into English from Scotus's simple but inelegant scholastic Latin. Despite these drawbacks, none deny his importance to theological and philosophical speculation; because of these drawbacks, many are content to rely on caricatures of what he wrote. The result has been unfair neglect, at best. This is bad for scholarship but even worse for disseminating Scotus's ideas outside of academia. He deserves to be more widely known, and more widely understood. And those intellectually active people whose intellectual lives are not determined, or at least not wholly determined, by the conventions of the modern academy deserve a book which gives an approachable portrait of Scotus. But, because we know so few of the facts of Scotus's own life, we can only really approach the man through his mind. We do know that the early Franciscan movement was the nest in which this eagle of philosophical and theological speculation learned to fly. Therefore, while this study of Scotus is focused on ideas, I hope I have also done some justice to that evangelical ethos in which Scotus developed those ideas.

2
THE EXISTENCE OF GOD

Lord our God, truest Teacher, when your servant Moses asked for your name, that he might proclaim it to the children of Israel, you replied, knowing what the mind of mortals is able to conceive of you, revealing your blessed name: "*I am who I am.*" You are True Existence. You are Total Existence. This I believe, and this, if it is possible for me, I would like to know. Help me, Lord, as I seek the extent of the cognition it is possible to achieve by natural reason of the True Existence you are, if we begin with the *being* you have predicated of yourself.

—Bl. John Duns Scotus, *Tractatus de Primo Principio*

My advice to an ordinary religious man, supposing anyone were to desire my advice on this point, would be to avoid all arguments about religion, and especially about the existence of God. However, to those who know some philosophy I would recommend the study of Duns Scotus's proofs for the actual existence of an Infinite Being.... It is getting to be rather generally admitted that, for accuracy and depth and scope, this is the most perfect and complete and thorough proof for the existence of God that has ever been worked out by any man.

—Thomas Merton, *The Seven Story Mountain*

SIMPLE AND LEARNED

St. Francis of Assisi founded his Order of Friars Minor in 1209. Fifteen years later, Bl. Agnellus of Pisa and a few of his Franciscan brothers landed at Dover, less than a week before their holy founder received the stigmata on Mt. Alverna. Within a year there were Franciscan communities at Canterbury, London, and Oxford—the spiritual, political, and intellectual centers of England, respectively. Within a decade Franciscan houses were established in most of the cathedral towns of England, and a few in

Scotland and Wales. And by the late 1250s there were about 1,250 friars in 250 communities of the English Franciscan province. In the late 1270s a man named Elias was head of the Franciscan house at Dumfries. Some records indicate that Elias came from a village called Duns, in Berwickshire, and was the uncle of a boy named John, also from Duns, who was born in 1265 or 1266. We know hardly anything about this boy except that he joined the Franciscans, by some accounts at Uncle Elias's own house at Dumfries, and later went up to Oxford, probably at the young age of thirteen, to study the liberal arts and the Bible.

At Oxford he lived at the Franciscan house, reading in its library, praying in its chapel, eating in its refectory. Only a wall remains today of that Franciscan dwelling: where Scotus lived and prayed and had his profoundest thoughts, there is now a shopping mall. The earliest Oxford Franciscans could not have envisioned a fall so low as for their sacred foundations to prop up such modern monuments of consumer culture as Marks & Spencer and Topman. Back then, their greatest concern was that young members, inspired by the Franciscan rule but still badly formed, would abandon the way of evangelical poverty in favor of unholy intellectual pursuits. Once, Bl. Agnellus walked into the seminar room while some brothers sat in philosophical disputation. To his horror he realized they were debating whether God exists. "Simple brothers enter Heaven, and learned brothers dispute whether there is a God at all!" he lamented.

Agnellus's solution to his brothers' inquisitiveness would prove monumentally important: rather than force a retreat from intellectual affairs, he entrusted their intellectual formation to Robert Grosseteste, later bishop of Lincoln, and the greatest Oxford scholar of the day. The chronicler Thomas Eccleston reports that under Grosseteste's care the brothers "made incalculable progress both in scholastic disputations and in the subtle moralities suitable for preaching."

Due to Agnellus's pastoral care and Grosseteste's intellectual care, the Franciscan house in Oxford was, by the time Scotus arrived some fifty years later, a setting in which the young Franciscan could safely investigate whether indeed God exists, not in the skeptical spirit which made Agnellus so fretful, but in the Augustinian and Anselmian spirit of *faith seeking understanding*. Scotus, as well as anyone in his order, showed that it was possible to be both a simple brother who enters heaven and a learned brother who disputes whether God exists.

REASON'S LIMITS

Blessed John's investigation of God's existence is unsurpassed in creativity and rigor. He did indeed think that reason could demonstrate, so as to make it a matter of knowledge, that God exists. Despite this confidence in reason, however, Scotus carefully circumscribed the range of reason's power to get to God. The knowledge of God most worth having, Scotus affirmed, is knowledge only God can give us. God made us, on purpose, to be creatures who could not in principle discover a rational route to eternal beatitude. God wanted it this way, so that He himself would be personally involved in our acquisition of the theological wisdom which discloses His vision for us and reveals how we can enjoy in turn the beatific vision.

All on our own, however, we *can* know that the end of our loving is not this or that good thing but the Good itself. We can know we cannot be truly happy unless we are somehow united in love with the Good. But what we cannot discover on our own is that this God who is the Good is a Trinity of Persons, and that God has made possible our eternal beatitude by drawing us into the divine life through the God-Man, Jesus Christ. Reason could never have guessed all this. Nevertheless, reason need not be caught completely off guard. It is the good news which could never have been guessed but, when revealed, somehow makes sense.

The Gospel can make sense to us in this way because the work of unaided human reason can, Scotus argues, get us all the way to a Supreme Nature with a Triple Primacy: the First Cause of everything besides itself, the Ultimate End of everything in the universe, and the Most Perfect nature possible. Reason can reveal that this Nature is also personal, that is, a thinker and a lover: mind and love stand at the back of all things. Reason here reaches its glass ceiling, and it is a dark glass. But illumined by revelation reason can peer upward, saying, "I knew it would be wonderful; I did not know it would be this wonderful."

FOR THE LOVE OF MYSTERY

But what is the point of reason's quest if it cannot reach the goal? What especially is the point for a young man already baptized, catechized, and confirmed, as Scotus himself surely was before he learned how to speculate metaphysically about God's existence and nature? Is not the labor of reason wasted on divine things, the revelation of the Gospel having already come to us?

No, reason is not wasted on divine things. While the well-formed Christian may not personally need philosophical theology in order to be persuaded about the truth of the Faith, he may still find it helpful in evangelistic efforts, helping others on their way to faith. But also, and more fundamentally, the work of philosophical theology is not in vain because we are made in God's image, and that image consists mainly in our personal powers of intellect and will. Using these powers to their utmost—thinking hard about the highest things, loving deeply the best things—is itself a God-honoring use of the talents we have been given. Moreover, love naturally seeks to know more about its beloved. As St. Augustine said in his book *On the Trinity*, we should seek to discover the unknown, not out of anxiety to unveil all mystery, but out of love for it, to be united with it. That knowledge which is the fruit of the love of mystery is wisdom—in contrast to that mere curiosity which is the knowledge gained by making war on mystery.

But while philosophical reasoning about divine things is a natural human enterprise, we are not all equally good at it. It is difficult to do well, even if we agree with St. Paul that the invisible nature of God has been clearly perceived by all men in the visible things God has made (Rom 1:20). Each of us, then, is a little natural theologian. Apprenticing ourselves to great natural theologians—and Duns Scotus is among the greatest—is a helpful way for us small ones to grow in the knowledge love can reveal, and to express our love to the One who has given us our minds.

POSSIBLE EXISTENCE

Duns Scotus's rational route to God begins, oddly enough, with the Bible. God revealed himself to Moses as "I am who I am," and for most of Christian theological history theologians have thought this self-disclosure means that God is, somehow or other, Existence itself, or the sole ultimate explanation of the whole of existence. "You revealed yourself to Moses as 'I am who I am.' You are true existence. You are total existence. This I believe and this I seek to know, if it is possible for me to know it." So begins Scotus's *Treatise on the First Principle,* one of the most powerful works of natural theology ever written.

Scotus's strategy is to reflect on the very nature of existence, because in doing so he thinks he can show that God exists. If it is even just *possible* for something to exist, it follows that God *must* exist. Suppose that nothing whatsoever exists. In such a circumstance, it would not be possible for something to begin to exist. This is because nothing can cause itself to exist, and, in our imaginary scenario, there is nothing else around to cause something to exist. So if there is nothing at all, then necessarily there will always be nothing at all. Now, in fact we know that it is possible for something to begin to exist. We know this because some things did in fact begin to exist. The actual existence of these things is then the source of our knowledge that it is possible for something to begin to exist. But only our *knowledge* of that possibility, not the *possibility itself*, depends on there being any actual things which began to exist. That possibility is instead a necessary condition for anything beginning to exist—after all, if it were not possible for something to begin to exist, then there would be nothing which began to exist. So the possibility that something begins to exist is part of the explanation of why there are things which have begun to exist, while conversely, the fact that things have begun to exist does not in any way explain why it is possible for something to begin to exist. Thus, while we know that it is possible for something to come into existence only because there are in fact some things which began to exist, we can also know that these existing things cannot explain *why* it is possible for something to come into existence.

So we know that something can come into existence. Moreover, we can think about something which can come into existence, while disregarding the fact that it exists, if it exists, or disregarding the fact that it does not exist, if it does not exist. We can think about it, and go on to consider what must be true about it, if we attend just to the fact that it is the sort of thing which *can* exist.

If this all sounds very abstract, here is a familiar example to show that this is not all as abstruse as it first seems. Think of Tolkien's myths and legends preserved in books like *The Lord of the Rings* and *The Silmarillion.* In particular, think of an orc, such as Grishnákh. In Tolkien's mythology, the orcs are a type of personal animal which has some sort of genealogical relationship to the elves. The Dark Lord

Morgoth tortured elves and corrupted them, and over many years in unknown ways produced from them the race of orcs. If we consider Grishnákh, we can think not only about his personality and personal appearance, but also about his provenance. That is, given that orcs are a kind of animal, we know that Grishnákh is descended in some way from orc parents. We also know that he depends for his ongoing life on things like the air of Middle Earth, water, food, the goodwill of the Valar, and ultimately on the goodwill of Illúvatar, who in Tolkien's mythology is the original source of everything besides himself. And we know Grishnákh can be destroyed, as he is destroyed when he is trampled and speared by the Riders of Rohan. We know that Grishnákh bears some sort of genealogical relationship to elves, even if we don't know how the Dark Lord brought about orcs from elves—by selective breeding or by genetic manipulation or in some other way, we just don't know. But we do know that orcs wouldn't have been if elves hadn't been. And elves wouldn't have been if the Valar hadn't made a world for them to be in, and if Illúvatar hadn't made the elves to be in that world. Thus, in thinking about a single orc we can come to see something of the wider web of dependencies that obtain in Middle Earth. And all these dependencies obtain even though, as we are sometimes unfortunate to recognize, Middle Earth and its creatures are not real. It's a world depicted with great vividness and depth, and so it feels to so many readers that it could or should be real. But it's not real, or at least it's not real as our world is real. Thus, in thinking about an orc in Middle Earth, we are thinking about a merely possible being, but even as a merely possible being the orc stands in so many relationships of dependence, and so we can also think about at least some of these other merely possible things the orc depends on.

The point of the example is to show that we really do have some acquaintance with the sort of thinking that

Scotus is asking us to do. He wants us to set aside for the moment that we know that so many of the things we think about are in fact real: tables, chairs, horses, cows, and so on. Ignore the fact that they're real, he's asking us. Think of all the things in the real world as though they made up one big fantasy world, like Tolkien's Middle Earth. Attend just to their *natures*, and in doing so you will see that there is nothing about their natures which demands that they exist, just as in considering the nature of Grishnákh we find nothing about him that demands that he exists. So if there really are tables and chairs and so on, these exist because *something else* has caused them to exist. More generally, we can see that if something can come into existence, then, should it begin to exist, it will do so as an effect of some cause. This is because it could not cause itself to exist. So something can come into existence only if something else can cause it to exist. Now think about this something else. If it too is the sort of thing which, if it exists, begins to exist, then it too exists only if something else causes it to exist. We can go through the same rational procedure with this new something else, with the same result: if it is yet a third thing which, if it exists, began to exist, then it too exists only if something else causes it to exist.

And now we're drawing close to our target. For what it would take for something to be able to begin to exist is for something that in fact exists to be able to cause it to exist. However many links there are in the chain of causes, none of them will actually exist unless there is something at the very back which already exists. The character Illúvatar is obviously like God in many ways, but he is unlike God in a very profound way: he doesn't make all the things he originates to be really real, real as tables and chairs and you and I are real. In the world of Tolkien's stories Illúvatar really is the first thing, but he is just as much a part of that merely imaginary world as

Grishnákh. So to explain the actual existence of things, we need a first thing with a feature Illúvatar clearly does not have, the feature of actually existing. But this one who Already Exists cannot itself have been caused to exist. After all, if it had been caused, then it began to exist. But we already know that this great Already did not begin to exist. It always was. And so it always was uncaused. It is in fact that most Actual Thing which is the necessary condition for there being any actual thing whatsoever that begins to exist.

ULTIMATE PURPOSE

But Scotus is far from done. He recognizes as well as you do that the God he loves is not some bland First Efficient Cause. Showing that there must be such a thing is therefore not in fact enough to reach God. So Scotus offers additional arguments to establish that this First Efficient Cause really is God. The first of these is that there is something in fact which is the ultimate purpose or *final cause* of the existence of anything which has a purpose. Purposes explain why things happen, so Scotus and his tradition were happy to say that they were a kind of cause. On Scotus's distinctive understanding, a purpose is a cause only when it somehow exists *before* the thing it is supposed to explain. The carpenter's idea of the cabinet, along with his desire to bring that idea into reality through the art of his carpentry and the oaken boards in his shop, explains why the cabinet now exists. That idea of the cabinet moves or motivates the carpenter to build, and therefore it factors into an overall explanation of the actual cabinet's existence, and is therefore one of its causes. It is called the "final" cause in the sense that it is the goal the carpenter aims to achieve in his carpentry. So Scotus's argument for a First Final Cause is therefore an argument that there is something for the sake of which things can come into existence—not just this cabinet or that egg salad, but everything whatsoever which can come into existence.

The goal or purpose of the cabinet-making explains the cabinet, as we have seen. Similarly, it seems, the goal or purpose of web-spinning explains the spider's web. We are strongly inclined to think that that particular activity of spinning occurs for that particular goal. In fact we even name the activity, spinning a web, after the goal, the web, which we are strongly inclined to think is the goal or purpose of that activity. But there is this funny difference between the web-spinning and the cabinet-making. With a few notable exceptions, such as Charlotte and Shelob, spiders cannot have their webs in mind when they spin them. But carpenters do have their cabinets in mind when they build them. In fact it is the cabinet in the carpenter's mind that explains how the finished cabinet is a cause of the cabinet-making. So if the web cannot exist in the spider's mind, how can the web be a cause of the spinning? One sort of answer is simply to deny that it is a cause of the spinning. A better answer is to affirm that it is indeed a cause of the spinning, but to look beyond the spider for an explanation of how it can be a cause of the spinning.

The carpenter gives us a clue about what to look for. For the spinning to be for the sake of the web, what we need is a mind for the web to be in. But we cannot find the mind in the spider. So we must look for it elsewhere. Now there are some familiar examples of minds, namely the minds of other people. When you look at the spider spinning, for example, in some sense you do have the web in mind. You know that what the spider is doing is bringing about a web, and in order to know this you need to have the web in mind. So webs do exist in minds. But our own minds are not the right minds for explaining why the spinning really is for the sake of the web. When we *know* that connection we are not *causing* that connection. It is a real connection out there in the world, waiting for us to discover it. What we need, then, is a mind which can not only hold the web, but make it the case that the web is a cause of the spinning. The sort of mind that can do this is the one with power to hold the web in mind, intend to make that web a reality, and then do what it takes to make that web a reality—say, by making the spider.

The web is just an example, of course, of a much wider aspect of the natural world. Countless things act for goals, but those goals can only be part of the explanations of those actions if those actions occur with a goal in mind. So this general feature of goal-directedness in the world requires some mind which not only beholds all the goals, but has the right kind of causal oversight of all those actions which are for the sake of goals. This brings us back to the carpenter, whose building is for the sake of the cabinet precisely because the carpenter has the cabinet in mind and is moved to build for the sake of the cabinet. We need something more than a carpenter which undertakes its building activity for the sake of the goals we find in nature. In pursuit of the First Final Cause, then, we learn something new about the First Efficient Cause, namely, that it must have or be a mind, the sort of thing which can have an idea about what it can cause and a will to direct its causal power to making the idea a reality outside itself, as the carpenter knows the cabinet and wills to make the cabinet a reality outside himself.

And now we're getting very close to the First Final Cause. World-building itself is an activity, the activity of the First Efficient Cause. Yes, this one activity is diverse in its effects, just as the one activity of cabinet-building involves many subsidiary activities with their subsidiary goals: measuring, cutting, nailing, gluing, clamping, staining, varnishing, and so on. But these little activities are all parts of the one big activity of cabinet building; and the little goals of each of these activities are all pursued for the sake of the one big goal of the cabinet. So too for world-building. Whatever it is for the sake of which the First Efficient Cause causes the world, that is the one Big Goal, the First Final Cause, of the Efficient Cause's world-building. And, like the First Efficient Cause, the First Final Cause cannot itself have been caused to exist. This is because it is that for the sake of which the First Efficient causes whatever it causes. It is, so to speak, already there, known and loved by the First Efficient, and for the love of which the First Efficient causes whatever it causes.

FIRST IN PERFECTION

But what is this Big Goal for the love of which the First Efficient Cause builds this little world? The answer requires us to turn our attention to Scotus's third sort of primacy, the primacy of Perfection. Scotus thinks there is such as a thing as the First in Perfection, and therefore thinks there is something most worthy of love. Since the First Efficient Cause is the source of all rationality and the wellspring of all love—all created persons are just so many copies of its intelligence and will—it will love most of all, and therefore act ultimately for the sake of, whatever is First in Perfection.

The argument that there is a thing that is First in Perfection begins from the premise that, considering the natures of things irrespective of whether they exist, some things are more perfect than others. The man who can run consecutive four-minute miles is a better runner than the one who can run consecutive seven-minute miles. The virtuous person is a better person than the vicious. A human being is a better thing than a charcoal briquette. Scotus thinks that what makes possible these objectively true judgments about the natures of things is some standard, a rule or measure by which we can judge things better or worse.

We have an idea of what makes for good running: speed and endurance are the most important characteristics, so the one who can run fast and far is a good runner, and the one who can run faster and farther than another is a *better* runner. Admittedly, we lack a concept of the best runner, but we can indirectly refer to what it would be: the concept of the runner who can transport himself by his own legs the fastest and the farthest that self-moved legs can move. Again, we have an idea of what makes for a good person: consistently excellent action that is characteristic of personal powers. Thus, a virtuous person is better than a vicious person in that the virtuous person wills and does the right thing consistently, with ease and delight in doing good, whereas the vicious person does not. Finally, we have even a concept of a good *thing*, and this is what makes sense of our judgment that a human being is better than a charcoal briquette, a judgment enshrined in instinct, common sense, moral theory, and the law. Things alive and capable of thinking and willing and feeling are better than things incapable of these actions.

The concept of the good thing is what is most important for understanding Scotus's reasons for thinking there is a Most Perfect nature. What he is going for here is something that is unqualifiedly better than any other kind of nature, no matter what. This Most Perfect nature is not the best so-and-so, or such-and-such, but the best possible thing, unqualifiedly. And a judgment like the judgment between humans and charcoal briquettes is the sort of judgment that reveals our intuition at least that there could be such a nature. After all, if judgments about better and worse make use of a standard, and if it makes as much sense to judge between *things* as it does between kinds of things like *runners* and *humans*, then we should be willing to grant the concept of a best or ultimate thing, the thing than which no thing could be greater, to adapt St. Anselm's famous phrase.

Now one aspect of the concept of the best possible thing is that it cannot be caused to exist. Scotus thinks this because to be caused to exist (e.g., by the First Efficient Cause) entails being caused to exist for some purpose (e.g., the First Final Cause). But anything which exists for the sake of something else is *less perfect* than the thing for the sake of which it exists. But then nothing existing for another's sake could be the greatest possible thing. It follows, then, that the Most Perfect thing is an uncaused thing. Thus, if it should turn out really to exist, it would exist on its own and not due to any cause. Now Scotus has already established that the First Efficient Cause and the First Final Cause are uncaused. Thus, if the Most Perfect thing did not exist, then it would be a nature surpassed in perfection by two things: they would have the perfection of being self-existent things, but the Most Perfect thing would not. But it is contradictory that the Most Perfect thing should be excelled by anything. Thus, given the existence of the First Efficient Cause and the First Final Cause, the existence of the First in Perfection follows.

FIRST, FINAL, AND BEST: THESE THREE ARE ONE

But Scotus does not think that there are in fact three self-existent natures. He thinks that one and the same divine nature is the self-existent thing which is all three: the First Efficient Cause, the First Final Cause, and the First in Perfection; to It alone belongs the Triple Primacy. And here, finally, we get to something recognizable as the God who is the object of our highest love. The argument, after all this hard work, is refreshingly simple. If there were two or more self-existent things, then they would have the property of self-existence in common. Then, as a matter of logic, either they would be dependent on this property for their self-existence or they would not. If they were dependent, then the self-existent natures would be dependent for their being self-existent on the property of self-existence. But then they wouldn't truly be self-existent natures, which is contradictory.

But something contradictory also follows if we suppose that they are not dependent for their self-existence on the property of self-existence—that having the property of self-existence is insufficient to make it the case that something self-exists. It would be fine if the property in question were something ordinary like being red: of course having the property of being red is insufficient to make it the case that some red thing exists—otherwise Santa Claus's redness would entail that he exists. But here we're dealing with a property the very meaning of which includes existence. So anything that has it exists, and self-exists. Either way then—whether or not we suppose that the property of self-existence is what self-existent things depend on for their self-existence—we run into contradictions if we assume there is more than one self-existent thing. But it has already been shown that the First Efficient is self-existent, the First Final is self-existent, and the First in Perfection is self-existent. Therefore we must conclude that all three are one and the same nature. These three do not *share* the property of self-existence; they are instead the one nature which *is* self-existence.

DIVINE SELF-LOVE

It is one thing to be forced to conclude that one nature has the Triple Primacy from the fact that at most one thing can be self-existent and that each of the Three Firsts is self-existent. It is another thing to try to glimpse the inner conceptual relations of these Three Firsts, to see a bit more directly why the identification of all three as one nature makes sense. Scotus himself called his theorem asserting the Triple Primacy a "most fertile" conclusion, and for good reason. Dwelling on God's Triple Primacy can lead us from glory to glory of contemplation. God, the First Efficient Cause, loves God, First in Perfection, above all; God, First in Perfection, is himself the First Final Cause of all that God, the First Efficient Cause, causes. And we would not want God to have acted differently! For it belongs to the excellence of a will to love best what is most worthy of love, and God who is First in Perfection is by nature the most worthy of love.

God's activity, then, is always tied up with his perfect self-love. And this activity includes any efficient causal activity, whereby God makes finite things into a created world. God efficiently causes the world out of love for himself, willing each and every stage of history, each and every thing in the world, from the most exalted archangel to the dullest grain of sand, for his own sake. The purpose each of us has is the purpose we have been given as a way in which God loves himself. Selfishness in us is vicious because we are infinitely lower than the First in Perfection: it is wrong for us to will our own good as if we were the most lovable things. But it is right for God so to will himself because He is the most lovable thing.

But consider how many ways God could have loved himself perfectly! God need not have created a world at all. The Father, Son, and Holy Spirit really are enough for each other. And, given God's choice to make a world, it could have been ordered infinitely many different ways and still have been equally a perfect act of God's self-love. But God chose this world, this history, these critters, you and me, as the token of his love for himself. A man buys a ring for his bride, and of course the bride is infinitely more precious than the ring. But precisely because of his love for his bride, he loves the ring, he wants it to please her, he will have it be beautiful, precious, a true token of his beloved. That token is what we are. We have been chosen to be God's gift of love to himself, and in being chosen we too are loved.

3

SPEAKING OF GOD

> Lest there be a dispute about the name "univocation," I designate that concept univocal which possesses sufficient unity in itself, so that to affirm and deny it of one and the same thing would be a contradiction. It also has sufficient unity to serve as the middle term of a syllogism, so that wherever two extremes are united by a middle term that is one in this way, we may conclude to the union of the two extremes among themselves.
>
> —Bl. John Duns Scotus, *Ordinatio*

> Neither is all predication purely equivocal, as some have said, since this would entail that nothing can be known or demonstrated about God, but rather would always be subject to the fallacy of equivocation. This would be contrary to the philosophers, who prove many things about God through demonstration.
>
> —St. Thomas Aquinas, *Summa theologiae*

STABLE MEANING

So far we have said a lot about God. And because we have been examining what Scotus thinks we can know about God by natural reason alone, we have made heavy use of *arguments*: rigorous discourse which proceeds through premises we already know to conclusions we can discover. Good arguments demand stable meanings of terms. If a term in a conclusion looks and sounds the same as a term in a premise, but has a different meaning, then even if the conclusion is true, we can't know it is true on the basis of that muddy argument. It's hard to keep our meanings stable in this way, and this is part of what makes philosophy in general so difficult, let alone the sort of philosophy which seeks what can be known about God. But this difficulty is not unique to philosophy. The struggle for stability of meaning across several occurrences of a word in an argument is but the philosopher's peculiar mode of our common human struggle with words. Poets know the struggle too; they know, no less than philosophers, that "Words strain, / Crack and sometimes break, under the burden, / Under the tension, slip, slide, perish, / Decay with imprecision, will not stay in place, / Will not stay still." In these lines from the *Four Quartets*, T. S. Eliot blames the decay of words not so much on bad thinking as on bad character. Words are "assailed" by the "Shrieking voices, / Scolding, mocking, or merely chattering." The assault on words is so wrong, and so dangerous, because, for rational animals living in space and time, words are the means to "reach / Into the silence." And it is "Only by the form, the pattern," that our words can "reach / The stillness." What is this silence, this stillness? It is "the still point of the turning world," the fixed eternal thing which makes it so that the past is never truly lost, and the future never completely unknown. By means of words we can strive toward this divine reality. As we have seen, Scotus thinks that the most important words are given to us by God himself, in the form or pattern of Holy Scripture and the teaching of the Church. But he likewise thought that the words we use in philosophy can also be of use in our striving toward the eternal God, and the form or pattern the philosopher's words must take is set by the canons of logic, and the canons of logic demand stable meanings.

The rule of logic is after all a necessary condition for genuine religious affection, poetic insight, and mystical ascent. It is the knowledge of *something* about the Beloved that lures the mystic out into darkness to seek Him, or that works upon the poet's imaginative powers. To be sure, when God is the Beloved there will always be infinity withheld, however high the ascent or however deep the insight. But the coyness intrinsic to Infinite Being does not imply that we know nothing about God as He really is. And our abilities to pursue the Infinite Being in thought and in love do imply that we must be able to say something precise, accurate, and positive about It. There have been and, alas, there continue to be some theologians who insist we can only ever say what God is not. To these Scotus replies, "The object of our greatest love is not a negation." The context in which he penned these words makes them inescapably polemical, and as polemic they constitute the greatest one-liner in all of Scholasticism. But the line is so succinct and so weighty, so much in contrast to the prolix arguments surrounding it, that it feels much more like a declaration of intimacy than a postulation of a thesis.

In a course of lectures on the *Sentences*, Peter Lombard's famous theology textbook, Blessed John was expected to offer his opinion on one of the introductory topics of the book, namely, what sort of knowledge we can have of God in this life, apart from revelation. In the relevant chapter, he would have read quotations from St. Paul, St. Ambrose, and St. Augustine, asserting that God's existence and nature can be known through careful reflection on what we know about creatures. He would have read there also that this careful reflection reveals just how radically different God must be from anything we know through our senses. So there are these extremes: on the one hand that creatures make God's existence and nature evident, and on the other hand that God, so to speak, is definitely not in the normal run of things.

UNIVOCITY AND LOGIC

Scotus's bridge between the extremes is his famous—sadly, and unjustly, infamous—theory of the univocity of the concept of being. Fundamentally, the theory is meant to explain how it is that God can be approached by our intellects in rational argumentation, and how He can be approached in love by our restless hearts. The central insight of the theory is that the standards for good reasoning about God are exactly the same standards for good reasoning about anything. Piety does not excuse fallacies. The theory of univocity holds that some of our words mean exactly the same thing when used of God as they mean when used of creatures. Here's an illustration. The following line of reasoning is valid and, I fancy, sound:

1. Any perfection of an effect is also a perfection of the cause of that effect.
2. God is the cause of the universe.
3. The universe includes the perfection of being good.
4. Ergo, God is good.

It's undoubtedly a valid argument, but we needn't get bogged down with the technical explanation of its validity. Whether or not it is a *sound* argument, truly proving that God is good, is a topic for another time. For now, just consider how the argument is supposed to yield its conclusion. It tells us that the cause of an effect has the same perfections as the effect. Maybe it has more perfections, maybe it has the perfections the effect has in greater (or lesser) degrees, maybe it is related to its perfections in a different way, but the argument itself doesn't tell us any more than that the cause of an effect has the perfections its effect has. Then, since the universe has these perfections, we can deduce that God has these perfections too.

All this is elementary logic, with which no philosopher or theologian could disagree. But this is really all that Scotus's infamous theory amounts to. To repeat, the theory of univocity is a theory about how our words work when we talk about God, which is meant to explain how we can reason deductively about divine things, as the above argument does. It explains this by insisting that the words we end up attributing to God, in the conclusion of any deductive argument which attributes the same words to creatures, must have exactly the same meaning when attributed to God as they have when attributed to creatures. Put like this, we can see that Scotus's theory is in no way innovative. It is simply an assertion of the common knowledge that deductive arguments don't work when terms are used ambiguously. Terms that sound "equal" but have different meanings—"equivocal" terms, to use the technical expression—don't make for good arguments.

BEING BEFORE GOD?

Why, then, is Scotus's doctrine of univocity so controversial? The long answer to this question has been offered expertly in recent years by scholars such as Richard Cross and Thomas Williams, and there is no need to rehearse it here. The short answer is that various people have misunderstood Scotus. Some have thought that the doctrine of univocity applies to things in general rather than only to words and concepts. Whereas Scotus's actual view is that the concept or term "being" is used the same way for both God and creatures, others have claimed that his view instead is that God and creatures are beings in the same way. Those who misunderstand Scotus in this way sometimes go on to saddle him with the nefarious view that being is a thing or property that both God and creatures share. Having set up the straw man, they go on to accuse Scotus of very bad things, such as *idolatry*. After all, on the nefarious view, being is more fundamental than God himself; being turns out to be the ultimate explanatory principle of all things, even God himself.

Thank God, then, that Bl. John held no such view! Instead, he thinks that we really can isolate in our thinking a *concept* of being as such, being with no determining features added on to it. This concept of being is the fundamental intelligible link between God and creatures, by which we are able, really able, to leap in thought out of the realm of the world and into God Himself. Creatures are beings. God is the cause of creatures. Whatever is in the effect is also in the cause. So God is a being. Admittedly, it is prosaic almost to the point of irreverence to say about God merely that He is a being. But it is no less true for being prosaic, and the truth can never truly be irreverent, for God is Truth.

Still, many would balk at this assertion that God is a being. They think it entails that God is just one being among many, that calling God a being brings Him down to the level of mere creatures. While the piety on display in these sorts of protestations is admirable, the protests rest on a huge mistake. It simply does not follow that God is at our level if He is a being. Scotus would be the first to insist that God is *infinite being*, whereas any creature is merely a *finite being*. And there cannot be a greater gap between beings than infinite on one side and finite on the other. But even infinite being and finite being are exactly similar to one another in one tiny respect, a tiny respect which secures the whole of natural theology: each is a being. They do not share being, though creatures participate in God's being as effects participate in their causes, and as images participate in their exemplars. But we who think about beings have one simple concept—the concept of being—and we can correctly apply this very concept both to God and to creatures, to infinite being and finite being.

AQUINAS AND ANALOGY

There is an old rivalry between Dominicans and Franciscans on various points of theology and philosophy. The rivalry matters less today, as these orders have declined in numbers and influence; as their respective intellectual and religious cultures do not easily come into contact as they once did when they were prominent participants in the great universities of Europe; and, most importantly, as the widespread secularization of many parts of the world urgently demands an evangelical emphasis on the things these rivals hold in common.

But long ago the rivalry was not moribund, and certainly not completely petty. What began more or less as administrative turf wars had, by the 1270s, erupted into serious intellectual dispute. In 1277, the Dominican Robert Kilwardby published the *Condemnations*, in which various theses of Aristotelian and Arabic philosophy were judged to be incompatible with the Christian faith. Among the condemned propositions were some endorsed by Aquinas himself. The following year the Franciscan William de la Mare, who had studied with St. Bonaventure in Paris but now was teaching at Oxford, published the *Correction of Brother Thomas*, which featured a long list of theses pulled from Aquinas's *Summa theologiae*, together with William's attempt to refute each one. From the Franciscan point of view the *Correction* was a success, and was adopted by the English Franciscan province in 1282 as part of its theological curriculum, to be read as a sort of antidote while studying the suspect works of Brother Thomas. Then, in 1284 the new Archbishop of Canterbury, the Franciscan John Pecham, reissued his predecessor's *Condemnations*, making it clear that the Oxford Dominicans were their primary target.

Now, the problem here is that William de la Mare was a world-class scholar of biblical languages, but as a philosopher and a reader of philosophical texts he was, so to speak, at sea. He botched the *Correction*, and it should never have been adopted as a Franciscan textbook. Since it was full of misinterpretations of Aquinas and Aristotle, and since it was obviously the work of an incompetent philosopher, Dominicans were gifted with the most delightful of polemical harvests: picking off the low-hanging fruit. A few years after the *Correction* came out, a team of Dominicans published the *Correction of the Corrupter of Brother Thomas*. The battle lines had been drawn; the sour spirit of the battle had descended, and the jockeying and quarreling of the sons of Sts. Dominic and Francis would go on, for centuries.

There is a reason for this reminiscence about mendicant bellicosity here in a chapter on Duns Scotus's philosophy of language about God. The reason is that a second major reason Scotus's doctrine of univocity has been deemed a threat to theology is that St. Thomas Aquinas explicitly rejects univocity in favor of what he calls an "analogical" theory of how our words and concepts apply to God. This appears on the surface to be a deep disagreement between the greatest Franciscan philosopher and the greatest Dominican philosopher. And it is the latter, not the former, who is the greatest theologian of the Church. But what needs to be said here is, first, that incompetent and overwrought as William de la Mare's *Correction* was, it registered no quibble with Aquinas's doctrine of analogy, suggesting that there was no general Franciscan concern that Aquinas's doctrine spelled doom for natural theology. And second, there is no substantive opposition between the analogical view advanced by Aquinas and the univocal view advanced by Scotus.

The reason this merely verbal disagreement between Aquinas and Scotus has generated such controversy over the years is precisely because it appears—in its stark surface contradiction—to pit the best of the best of these rival groups against each other, a single combat to settle the battle. And in 1914 the single combat seemed to have been settled. For it was in this year of violence, on June 29, 1914, that Pope St. Pius X declared Thomism the philosophical foundation of the Church's theology. Eight days later, on July 27, 1914, he supplemented the decree with twenty-four discrete Thomistic propositions, intended to clarify just what the pope meant by the word "Thomism." (World War I began on July 28, 1914.) The fourth of these twenty-four theses says this: "Being... is not said univocally of God and creatures, neither equivocally, but analogically. . . ."

It is illuminating to imagine what Scotus might have thought as he looked down from heaven on Pius's propositions, especially the fourth. I imagine that subtle mind, serene and supercharged in the presence of God, reading Proposition Four and then mentally crafting a commentary which would begin like this: "'Univocal' is not a univocal term." The fact is that there is very deep concord between Aquinas and Scotus on this point of language about God, and the widespread misunderstanding of this supposed debate has a lot to do with the fact that words like "univocity" and "analogy" are not always used univocally. To get a sense of what Aquinas means by analogy, the most important thing to observe is that Aquinas is very careful to tell us what his analogical theory does and does not imply about how words work when we reason about God. Most importantly, Aquinas tells us that, whatever else his theory of analogy amounts to, it is the view that when we reason deductively from premises about creatures to conclusions about the Creator, the meaning of the relevant terms is sufficiently unified so as to preserve validity. Analogical terms do not have equivocal meanings. Thus, Aquinas affirms the central feature of Scotus's doctrine of univocity, the one feature of the doctrine that Scotus really seems to have cared about.

Nevertheless, a keen observer might reply, Aquinas explicitly rejects univocity! He does, but remember, "univocity" is not a univocal term, which we can see by noticing that what Scotus means by "univocity" is simply not what Aquinas means. If I use "leg" to mean "leg or tail" and you use "leg" to mean "leg," and I say the dog has five legs and you say four, then we have no substantive disagreement. We have a semantic disagreement, which you can resolve by quoting some Abraham Lincoln to me. On the question of univocity, the disagreement between

Scotus and Aquinas is largely semantic. For Scotus, all it means for terms to be univocal is for them to be sufficiently similar in meaning to preserve validity in deductive reasoning. And Aquinas agrees that we can reason about God validly, and acknowledges that a condition for valid reasoning—about anything, God included—is unity of meaning across occurrences of the relevant terms in arguments. But this is not what Aquinas calls univocity.

Instead, Aquinas rejects univocity in the sense which has to do with the relationship between some *causes* and their *effects*. In this alternative sense, *things* are univocal when a cause produces an effect of the same nature as itself. Thus, human parents are *univocal causes* of their offspring, because both parents and offspring are human. But God is not a univocal cause of creatures, because any creature whatsoever, and all creatures taken together, have natures different from the divine nature. From this non-univocal feature of the causal connection between God and creatures, Aquinas infers that the words we use to talk about God and creatures are themselves non-univocal. For example, Aquinas is happy to say that both God and some creatures are wise. But he thinks wisdom as applied to creatures is not univocal with wisdom as applied to God. And he offers one main reason for thinking this. God is not related to wisdom the same way we are: God is identical with wisdom, whereas human beings have wisdom only as a quality which they can acquire or lose. But this means that "wisdom" as said of God somehow signifies the whole of what God is. As said of God, therefore, "wisdom" describes something—God himself—which exceeds all meaning we are actually able to understand when we use the term "wisdom." Therefore "wisdom" said of God has some difference from "wisdom" said of creatures, the difference of exceeding. But despite the difference, "wisdom" applied to either retains sufficient unity to be used in deductive arguments.

Here is the amazing thing: Duns Scotus would agree with nearly all of this. He would agree, for example, that God is simple, and so is the same as his wisdom. "Wisdom" as applied to God therefore signifies God. No wise creature is related to its wisdom in this divine way, so "wisdom" applied to a creature does not signify the whole creature itself. "Wisdom" as applied to God, therefore, really does signify something which exceeds the signification of "wisdom" as applied to a creature. What Scotus insists on, however, is that despite the difference which holds between these two uses of "wisdom," the meaning of the word remains sufficiently unified to preserve validity in arguments which proceed from creaturely wisdom to divine wisdom. And remember, when a word has this sufficient unity in an argument, that very fact is enough to make the word univocal, as Scotus understands univocity.

Aquinas also thinks that the meaning of "wisdom" across these two uses remains sufficiently unified to enable valid reasoning from creaturely wisdom to divine wisdom. But Aquinas understands univocity to be something more than this sufficient unity of meaning. And it is this something more which leads him to reject univocity as he understands it. What explains the one's rejection of univocity and the other's acceptance of it, therefore, is not substantive disagreement about any topic of real theological concern, but instead just their different views about what someone would be accepting or rejecting by accepting or rejecting a theory of univocity. Aquinas thinks accepting a theory of univocity would commit him also to accepting a view about causation according to which creatures have the same nature as God, just as offspring have the same nature as their parents. And no right-minded Christian theologian would want to embrace such a crazy view. No wonder, then, that Aquinas denied univocity, given his understanding of what univocity amounted to. But Scotus simply had a different understanding of what it meant to embrace the theory of univocity, an understanding which had nothing whatever to do with a view about the causal relationship between God and creatures. It's not that Scotus was uninterested in that causal relationship; it's just that, as he understood univocity, it did not entail any particular view about that relationship.

THE PARTICIPATION OF ALL CREATURES IN GOD

It is my hope that this comparison between Aquinas and Scotus will contribute in some small way to healing in those religious circles in which Scotus's univocity theory has been a cause of undue scandal. But I would like to dig a bit deeper, and say something about the practical payoff of the theoretical labor of articulating a theory about how our words work when we use them to talk about God. The fact is that we come to know what God is by coming to know what creatures are like. I can form a conception of God's love, by which I recognize in part why God is worthy of worship, from my experience of love from other people—parents, spouse, children, friends, and so on. Good philosophical theology eventually leads me to recognize that God's love is infinitely greater than the love of the greatest earthly lover. But univocity is the thread which tethers my concept of earthly love to heaven, and makes it reasonable for me to infer that love itself is perfected and without limit in God who is Love. Moreover, once it is recognized that God's love is infinite, indeed, that God is Love itself, we can go on to say true things about what this Love is, or must be, or may be, or could not be. Emphatically, we do not discover, at the end of reasoning about the nature of love, that God's love must be something different in kind from the love that we know from creatures. Love is love whether that love is infinite or finite. The difference between God's love and the earthly lover's is much more like a difference in degree. If it were different in kind, we would not know what we are talking about when we talk about God's love, or praise God for his love. This difference, however, is not *merely* a difference in degree. After all, God's Love is the exemplar of all other loves, and their causal origin, and that to which all other loves are ultimately ordered. We can know all this by revelation, and also by philosophical reflection on what God's Triple Primacy entails.

Scotus has been accused of dismantling a Christian metaphysics in which creatures participate in God. This is unjust. In fact he helped to maintain a worldview of the participation of creatures in God, and a deeper understanding of what it means, or at least should mean, for creatures to participate in God. This participation cannot mean that creatures are parts of God, God's body, or God's thoughts. Nor can it mean that God and creatures share some features in common, such as a Love which is something different from God and different from creatures but which is the Love which both God and creatures have insofar as they are loving. No, the truly Christian account of the participation of creatures in God is that God is the archetype of all creaturely perfections. There is nothing truly real in the realm of created being which is not also a mirror in which we can glimpse some aspect of God. Univocity—as Scotus understood univocity—uniquely supports this foundational aspect of the Christian doctrine of creation, assuring us that the concepts we form from our acquaintance with creatures are representing not only the creatures which produce those concepts, but some small aspects of the God who made those creatures.

■ 4

THE BIGGEST BIG QUESTION

In God the *logoi* of all things are steadfastly fixed, and it is on the basis of these that God is said to know *all things before they come into being,* for in absolute truth, in Him and with Him are all things, even though all things—things present and things to come—were not called into existence simultaneously with their *logoi* or with their being known by God. Instead, in the wisdom of the Creator, individual things were created at the appropriate moment in time, in a manner consistent with their *logoi*, and thus they received in themselves actual existence as beings.
—St. Maximos the Confessor, *Ambiguum*

God did not make man according to the same reason as the ass; therefore each has its own reason, and proper to itself. Also, these reasons are not external to God, because He does not need anything other than himself. Therefore they are in the divine mind. Also, it is only eternal things that exist in the divine mind. But the idea is in the divine mind. Therefore the idea is an eternal reason.
—Bl. John Duns Scotus, *Reportatio*

What happens in the writer's mind is something like this. When making a character he in a manner separates and incarnates a part of his own living mind.
—Dorothy L. Sayers, *The Mind of the Maker*

THE FAMILIARITY OF CREATION

The affinity of St. Francis for all creatures arose from his familiarity with creatures. Affinity for natural things arises in other ways, too. A Romantic's sense of sublime longing, or a mystic's sense of mystery, or even a sportsman's sense of adventure, gives rise to deep affinities for natural things. But Francis loved the wolf the way a man loves his wayward but likable brother, and he loved the birds as a Sunday School teacher loves her pupils. Stars and the elemental powers of nature are so many brothers and sisters, would-be Franciscans and Clarisses, if only there were habits big enough for them. Francis, who so adored the baby Jesus and his mother, Mary, could non-idolatrously feel the earth itself as a mother and himself as its nursling, never forgetting how much higher up the ladder even of created being the rungs of maternity and paternity ascend.

Francis felt this deep filial piety for all nature because he recognized the universal Fatherhood of God. A child might feel awe for an older sibling from time to time. But when big brother or big sister is receiving a lesson or rebuke from Mom and Dad, the awfulness is somewhat abated. Before Mom and Dad, all siblings are as children. Even so, the Sun and Moon, and the Wind, Water, Fire, and Earth, are all awesome. But if we can see with the eyes of Francis we see them in their proper places: not kings and queens but children and servants of the same Father.

The familiarity of the realm of nature therefore directs us to its Paterfamilias, and it was practically a religious revolution in the second millennium BC when the children of Abraham taught their children that God is the Father of all but has no spouse. God is the one origin of all things, their sole ultimate explanation, and therefore more truly is Father than any earthly father—human, animal, sidereal—can be. In this chapter I want to explore in some depth how Francis's disciple Blessed John thought about the origination of all things from God. And in this exploration I want to focus on one peculiar aspect of God's originality, one which I can think of no better way of introducing than by raising a question my eldest daughter once asked me at the zoo.

WHY ARE THERE GIRAFFES?

Every parent knows what it's like not to be able to answer "why" questions. My kids ask me "why" about all sorts of things I have no clue about; sometimes I fake an answer, sometimes I say I just don't know, and sometimes I tell them to ask Mom. And sometimes I do philosophy. The following is a real-life exchange I had with my eldest when she was two, during a trip to the zoo:

E: Daddy, what are those?
D: Those are giraffes.
E: Why?
D: . . .

How can we answer a question like this? Perhaps we can write off her answer as so many linguistic philosophers from the previous century would write it off: oh, well, she just doesn't understand the rules for the correct use of the term "why." But why would any sane person think this? Nine times out of ten her "why" question is perfectly normal and valid. Why, in the weird case, should we infer that it is she who misunderstands?

No, we must take the question seriously. Why are giraffes giraffes? That is a hard question! One way to answer her would be to introduce the concept of "tautology," and explain that if a giraffe is a giraffe, then it is a giraffe, and that's why giraffes are giraffes. But this clearly doesn't get us very far. And it isn't a fair answer, because she's not asking a question about how words work. She's asking a question about *giraffes.* So to respect her question, we must look deeper than logic. Why are giraffes giraffes? Does she mean, "Why are these things here in front of us, these very things causing me to point and laugh and kick my feet, why are these giraffes and not something else?" Or maybe, "Why are there giraffes at all? In this carnival world I'm beginning to explore, why should there be such creatures as these, so huge, so nightmarish in shape but so likable in bearing? Why are there giraffes?"

Since I cannot yet discern the precise sense of her question, let me comment on both candidates in turn. Why are these things giraffes rather than some other kind of thing? Here she's asking a question about individuals. Is it possible that one and the same thing be an altogether different kind of thing? Is it possible that a giraffe be a hippopotamus, or an orangutan, or a stone? And this is exactly the sort of question that receives an answer in the story of the Frog Prince. If a Prince can become a frog, then why shouldn't a giraffe be able to become a girl? The metaphysical assumption at play here is that one and the same thing can go on existing even if it changes its species. Of course, this isn't the only answer; still less is it the most common or the most obvious answer. A different, rather more traditional answer is this: no, actually, the giraffe cannot become a girl; I mean, by magic the giraffe might transform into a girl, but then that giraffe would cease to exist and a new thing, a girl, would begin to exist. The assumptions in the background to this traditional answer are that everything which exists exists as a certain kind of thing, and nothing can change its kind and still be the very thing that it is. So agree Roald Dahl and Wes Anderson in *The Fantastic Mr. Fox*: the whole point of that tale is that you can only be comfortable in your own skin by embracing not just who, but what, you really are.

Whether or not a giraffe can be something other than a giraffe is, of course, a question of immense importance for ethics and politics. But the correct answer to this question does not give us the right sort of answer to the other question, "Why are there giraffes at all?" And for now, it's this second question that counts. It's also a harder question. And it's the question I am inclined to think my daughter was really asking that day at the zoo. Had I more training in biology and less in philosophy and theology, I might have given her an account of the evolution of giraffes; but however sophisticated my answer along this line, it would not be a final answer. Evolutionary history does not put an end to reasonable "why" questions. And what we're looking for here—to quiet the kid, if nothing else—is the kind of answer that is ultimate: that, if true, ultimately explains why there are giraffes. This chapter is about Scotus's ultimate answer.

A REALLY BIG QUESTION

"Why is there something rather than nothing?" Here is one of the biggest of the Big Questions. But for all the deep philosophizing done in pursuit of answers to this question, it is not usually appreciated that the alternative to there being something is not, in fact, imaginable. I mean imaginable here in its literal sense—we can't form a mental picture of there being nothing at all. But I also mean imaginable in the stronger and broader sense: it is not thinkable, it is inconceivable. Suppose that it could have turned out that there is nothing at all, nothing rather than something. Well, then, had it turned out that way, it would be true *that there is nothing at all*. Not to pull a Pilate here—because I ask earnestly, not cynically—but what is truth? Or, better, what is *a truth*? For in that total circumstance in which we are supposing there is nothing rather than something, there turns out to be at least one truth, the truth that there is nothing at all. Now, what about this truth? Is it something, or nothing? Surely it is not nothing. If it were nothing, really nothing, it couldn't have any properties, such as being true. But it does—it's true! So in the circumstance in which there is nothing rather than something, there is in fact something, namely, the *truth* that there is nothing. But then the truth that there is nothing is not in fact true; it is in fact a falsehood. But if it is false that there is nothing, then there is something. So from the assumption that there is nothing at all, we can derive the contradiction that it is both true and false that there is nothing at all. But whatever is truly contradictory is not possible. So it is not possible that there is nothing at all, and it never has been possible that there could be nothing at all.

We're stuck with reality, and it's all we've got. But precisely because we're stuck with it, the Big Question about why there is something rather than nothing has never struck me as a very interesting question. The real question is not, after all, why there is something rather than nothing, but *why things are such as they are.* Why this way, and not some other way? Notice that we can imagine, in both the literal and broad senses, things being otherwise than they are. Thus, that they are this very way seems like the sort of fact which cries out for an explanation.

The explanation Scotus offers us has something to do with God, namely this: the world is as it is because it is the product of God's totally free creativity. God need not have made the world as it is. He need not have made a world at all. He could have made a world rather different from this one. So the contingency in things, which we recognize when we are moved to ask the Big Question about why things are such as they are, is due ultimately to divine freedom. Why are there giraffes? Because God wanted there to be giraffes.

THE BIGGEST BIG QUESTION

But even this doesn't give us the full ultimate explanation we seek, for the precocious child will go on wondering why giraffes are among the things God wanted. Before they got here on earth, how did they get There, in God's mind?

Now the quick reply is that they have always been in God's mind; there was never a time at which God had some ignorance to overcome, no giraffe-shaped hole in God's knowledge. But it would also be nice to have, if possible, some explanation why it is that, in God's eternal contemplation of the whole stock of his knowing, among the things he knows is the giraffe. It is no knock against the giraffe to marvel that it should eternally help to occupy God's thoughts. One answer, frequently associated with St. Thomas Aquinas, is that God knows about every kind of thing He could create, just by knowing himself perfectly.

If that sounds odd, consider this: *perfect* self-knowledge arguably would involve not just knowledge of oneself in isolation, but knowledge of oneself in relation to everything else. So if God is to be a perfect self-knower, then arguably He must know every way in which other things are related to Him. And among these relations would be relations such as imitation and similarity. God would know, let's say, exactly the way in which the giraffe is similar to Him. God's self-knowledge would therefore be partially made up of his knowledge of how the giraffe is a little imitation of God. And therefore God's idea of the giraffe would, in the end, be an idea of how God can be imitated.

Beautiful as this story is, it just does not hold water. To see this, notice that the giraffe can imitate God only if the giraffe is in some sense already there in God's mind as something to think about. It's because of what the giraffe is that it imitates God in the peculiar way it does. Granting the giraffe, we might be able to explain God's idea of it as an idea of himself. But in this context we're not granting the giraffe—we're trying to explain it. Moreover, we do not want to accuse God of knowing about the giraffe *merely* the way in which it imitates Him. After all, if it imitates God, then there is some way in which it is like God, but also some way in which it is not like God. If there weren't a way in which it wasn't like God, it would be the same as God. We might say that the Son and Holy Spirit are perfect images of the Father—perfect images because they're perfect imitations. But the giraffe is not a perfect imitation. Now since God knows everything, He would know the way in which the giraffe is not like Him. But then He would know something about the giraffe in addition to how the giraffe imitates him. So God's knowledge of all the ways He can be imitated cannot, in the end, successfully explain God's knowledge of the kinds of things He can create. If we want God's own thinking about himself to give us an explanation not just of how God knows what He can choose to make, but why it is there to be known in the first place, we must work a bit harder.

We are now in the deepest possible theological waters, and if you're like me you're not sure you *can* work any harder, when more than sufficiently occupied just trying to stay afloat and not drown. Scotus, fortunately, has done the hard work already, and is ready with the lifeboat. He saw exactly these weaknesses of the position associated with Aquinas. But he was extremely sympathetic to its basic outlines, so he did not discard the view altogether; he patched it up, to let it do what it was always supposed to do: give us the ultimate explanation of why there can be giraffes.

Here is Blessed John's patch. He grants that God, just by understanding himself, would thereby understand every possible thing He could create. And he grants that God, in understanding himself, would understand how every possible kind of creature imitates Him. But he does not think that God's knowledge of possible kinds of creatures has exactly the same content as his knowledge of the ways He can be imitated. Instead, Scotus thinks that God has ideas of possible kinds of creatures by understanding some limited facet or aspect of himself—directly, not by way of imitation. Of course, in knowing an aspect of his own nature, God would *then* understand how a possible creature imitates Him, since a possible creature really is a chip off the Old Block! But the foundational notion for Scotus is that *imitation comes after reality*, and the reality of a possible kind of creature is already there, contained in God, a facet of an infinitely-sided diamond.

Creation, therefore, amounts to God's free and artistic choice to express something of himself: limited, imperfect, yes; but genuinely imaging something of what God is, and therefore genuinely intimating to us, in our experience of the world around us, something of what God is. Daughter, why is there the giraffe? Because God wanted there to be giraffes, and giraffes were among the things for God to want, before there was anything else but God, because the giraffe is part of what God is. We therefore get to know something about God by getting to know the giraffe. And if God is the Highest Good and the one in the love of Whom we are blessed, then, Daughter, no wonder the giraffe brings you such joy.

GOD'S REASONS

But let us not get ahead of ourselves, easy as it is to do so in the service of so apt a philosopher as my daughter. We have treaded deep waters to try to answer the question how God has the ideas of creatures He has. But let us begin again with a closely related question, how God decides what to create, among infinite possibilities. The most emphatic thing to say here, on Scotus's behalf, is that creation is God's free choice. Neither reason nor goodness compels God to make anything—all the larks on a lark, all the legs just for kicks. That God has done so is because it pleased Him to do so. But, if we grant that God has decided to create just because it pleased Him to do so, we are not forced by either logic or piety to say that there is no explanation of why God chose to create this particular world. So let us begin again. How does God decide what to create, given his decision to create at all? We can think of God as an artist, having so many ideas and creatively ordering these ideas together into so many ideas of worlds. God sees in His mind all the worlds he could create. Maybe some are better than others, but all are good.

Some have thought there is a best. Leibniz is the most important representative of this sort of pious rationalism, though Plato adumbrated Leibniz's view long ago. And if there were a best, it would be hard to resist the rationalist view that God, who is all good, would be compelled by his goodness to create it, given his choice to create at all. But from the Scotist perspective, there could not possibly be a best possible world. It is part of the nature of any world to be finite. Thus, there couldn't be a best possible world, because, for any possible world with some finite degree of perfection, God could imagine another, at least slightly better. But then this possible worlds one-upmanship would never cease: God could always go on concocting better possible worlds.

Now even if there is no best world, it is not unreasonable to suppose that there is some rational procedure for God to go through by which to arrive at a good choice among all worlds. But this proves tricky. As a start, you might think that since all the worlds are good, a choice to create any of them would be a good choice. If we ask God's reason for choosing this world, we can say that He creates it because it is good. But this doesn't give us any information about why God preferred this world to all those other worlds, since the reason given for choosing this world, as far as it goes—"it's good"—is equally a reason for choosing all the other worlds. There is a similar problem with the supposition that God's reason for creating the world He creates is that it is better than the other worlds. This is because if, for any possible world, there is a better, then there is no world better than all other worlds God could create. For any world God decides to create, there will always be worlds better. This means that the reason from comparison—"it's better than those"—is also equally a reason for choosing many other worlds. So neither the goodness of a world nor its being better than other worlds are reasons that determine or specify which world of all the possibles gets created.

Maybe we could specify reasons a bit more. Let's say that God wants to create a world in which there are human beings. Clearly there are possible worlds which do not contain human beings—all this means is that God might have created a world in which there are no humans. So "it has human beings" is the sort of reason that rules out many worlds, since it does not apply to many worlds. But we're little helped with this restriction, since "it has human beings" will still be true of many worlds. While this reason narrows down the field, it doesn't narrow it down very much. So let's get even more specific. Let's say that God wants to create a world which includes you. But surely there are still many possible worlds God could have made which include you. So again, while it's true that we rule out very many worlds by saying that one of God's reasons for deciding which world to create is that "it has you in it," there are still many, many worlds we don't rule out.

But there is a deeper issue here. It's not just that "it has you in it" isn't the sort of reason that picks out just one world. The deeper issue is that it's not at all clear how a reason like "it has you in it" can be a reason for creating this world (or any world that includes you), as though this is a better reason than "it has Spanglebrook in it," where Spanglebrook is another human being who always remains a mere possibility. There is—and I do not mean to offend—nothing to distinguish you from Spanglebrook in a way that would make it more rational or better for God to create a world with you in it rather than a world which contains Spanglebrook. What Scotus would tell you is that there is no reason, no reason which determines God's choosing, to pick a world with you in it rather than a world with Comrade Spanglebrook. God just picks. This is the liberating yet terrifying answer: He just picks. God always acts for the good. But the good, in his case, does not determine a single course of action. Faced with limitless good possibilities, God simply picks one. But look: while this does mean that God acts arbitrarily, it does not mean that God acts for no reason. God does act for reasons. He just decides which reasons to act for. And this means that even if we do find a way to identify some list of reasons for creating a world which would leave exactly one world in contention, still, we must not think that that very list compels God to make this world. These reasons really would be the reasons for which God makes the world, and God couldn't have acted for just those reasons and made any other world. But He needn't have created for these reasons.

Now I think it's possible to list some reasons which really do uniquely pick out this world, such that if God were to act on these very reasons, this would be the world He would create. We know that this world that God creates is different in some way from all other possible worlds. No matter how similar two possible worlds might be to one another, one is bound to have at least one feature which the other lacks. What this world-distinguishing feature might be is hard to discern. It could be as easy as saying that two worlds are in every way alike except that one contains Spanglebrook and the other, alas, does not. Maybe there is some deeper, hidden feature, such that even if two worlds are in every other way alike, even in their containment of the elusive Spanglebrook, they are still to be distinguished by this hidden feature. In any case, we know that there is *something* about this world that sets it apart from all other worlds—not its goodness, not the fact that it contains humans, not even the fact that it contains you (since all these features are shared by other worlds)—but something. This world is unique. So if one of God's reasons for choosing this world is that it has whatever feature it is that makes it unique, then we've alighted upon a list of reasons that really do uniquely pick out this very world that God has made. This very list of reasons would pick out no other world. So if God had just this list of reasons for picking the world to make, this world would be picked.

This idea, that God acts arbitrarily in the sense that He decides what reasons to act for, seems to leave things rather unsettled. In fact it seems simply to back up the problem of how God gets his reasons for picking this world over all the other worlds He might make but doesn't. Let us grant this exotic thought that when God creates He creates for reasons, but that God is able to choose his own reasons. Still, the same sort of question arises: does God have reasons for choosing the reasons He chooses to create this world rather than other worlds? If our answer is that God has reasons for choosing his reasons, then we're back to where we started from, wondering how God decides on just these reasons for choosing these reasons. But if our answer instead is that God does not have reasons for choosing his reasons, then ultimately, at least some of God's actions are for no reasons—and in this case we might as well give up on the whole idea of God having reasons for choosing this world.

This is difficult. But here are some things I think we must say, and I think they are consistent with each other. First, God acts for reasons. Second, when it comes to creating or not creating, and when it comes to creating this or that, there are no reasons which compel God to do anything. Third, acting for reasons makes most sense when the reasons for acting pick out a unique course of action, distinct from other possible courses of action. Given these three commitments, we are bound to attribute to God the sort of freedom which lets Him pick this world because it is this very world. That it is this world, and no other, is God's reason for making it. This sublime thought lets every detail of this world, from the fallen sparrows to the individual hairs on your head—and much else besides—be among God's reasons for making this world. Of course there are much more important features of this world which are among God's reasons for making it—but that is a story for the final chapter. For now, we will continue to think about creation, moving from creation as an exemplar in God's mind to creation as the image of that exemplar.

5

THE CREATED ORDER

> It all seemed too good to be true. Hither and thither through the meadows he rambled busily, along the hedge-rows, across the copses, finding everywhere birds building, flowers budding, leaves thrusting—everything happy, and progressive, and occupied.
> —Kenneth Grahame, *The Wind in the Willows*

> The whole philosophy of St. Francis revolved around the idea of a new supernatural light on natural things, which meant the ultimate recovery not the ultimate refusal of natural things.
> —G. K. Chesterton, *St. Francis of Assisi*

> "He has no need at all of anything that is made. An eldil is not more needful to Him than a grain of the Dust: a peopled world no more needful than a world that is empty: but all needless alike, and what all add to Him is nothing. We also have no need of anything that is made. Love me, my brothers, for I am infinitely superfluous, and your love shall be like His, born neither of your need nor of my deserving, but a plain bounty. Blessed be He!"
> —C. S. Lewis, *Perelandra*

THE CHOIR OF CREATURES

God thinks eternally himself, a Trinity of persons self-sufficient, giving and enjoying. In the beauty of knowledge the Trinity beholds its own nature, the whole all at once, and every fact, and from all the facts God fashions so many ideas of worlds He might make. God alights in thought upon the idea of this world which is ours, loves it with a love that infinitely outstrips the degree to which it deserves to be loved—desires it so much that He makes it to have a reality of its own—not independent from Him, but other than Him.

The goodness of the created world is not such as to compel God, by some quasi-legal or moral obligation, to make it or to do one thing or another for it. God's goodness for us and for this world is a bounty, a mercy, and not the fulfillment of an obligation. This is why praise and thanksgiving are such natural and fitting attitudes for creatures like us to take up toward our Creator. St. Francis recognized this as well as anyone, and in the "Canticle of the Sun" he expressed his wish that God be praised through all creatures and not just his fellow human beings. The song is a simple way for us small ones to imagine the world as altogether ordered by love, the highest to the lowest all having a place in the choir of creation. Bl. John's philosophy of nature is his attempt to fill in the philosophical details of what the world must be like if it is the sort of world the "Canticle" describes.

PRINCIPLES OF NATURE

In his theorizing Scotus was, like every major philosopher of the thirteenth and fourteenth centuries, deeply inspired by Aristotle. Aristotle is the great philosopher of common sense, who sought as much as possible, when propounding a philosophical theory, "to preserve the phenomena," that is, to take common sense and everyday experience for granted, as good guides to truth. He recognized that certain absurdities follow if you suppose that the things we observe around us are made up *only* of particles, or atoms. On the atomistic understanding of nature, a thing like a dog is just a bunch of particles conglomerated; a thing like an oak tree is just a bunch of particles conglomerated. The precise ratio of particles of different kinds would be different for different things like dogs and oak trees, but the fundamental stuff of which they are made would be identical in kind. What this atomistic worldview inevitably leads to is a vision of nature in which natural things like dogs and trees are not fundamental. Descriptions of specifically doggy or treeish processes become, on this reductionistic worldview, mere shorthand for arrangements of particles floating in space. The changes whereby some doggy zygotes become a dog, or some dog dies and become a doggy corpse, are on this view, at the fundamental and most accurate level of analysis, purely spatial changes, just some particles changing their spatial locations.

Aristotle examined this worldview and found it wanting in some important details. In its attempt to explain what the dogs and the oaks really were it managed to explain away the dogs and the oaks. And while many reduction-minded scientists and philosophers throughout the ages would reckon this reduction a resounding success, Aristotle had the good sense to try for a theory which could leave rationally intact the unsurprising but apparently radical belief that, for example, dogs really do begin to exist when mommy and daddy doggies get together, and oak trees really do sprout from acorns. But in his efforts to keep hold of common sense in his philosophy of nature, Aristotle was forced by reason to embrace some principles of nature which, on the contemporary scientific worldview, do indeed surprise.

The most important innovative principle of Aristotle's natural philosophy is *form*. Form was Aristotle's attempt to explain what was different, at the fundamental level, between the oak and the dog. Recognizing that the material constituents of these very different organisms were not after all very different, Aristotle followed the data wherever it led and posited the principle of form as a non-material element which accounted for that difference. The dog and the oak may not differ much at the level of chemical analysis, and still less at the level of pure physics, but they do indeed differ, and that difference is form. The dog is not just its material parts; the oak is not just its material parts. The dog is in fact the composite of matter and dog form, and the oak is the composite of matter and oak form. These forms are supposed to explain the distinctive shape, way of growth, and characteristic life activities of the oaks and the dogs. The principle of form is generalizable to all organisms, including human beings, and to many non-living substances: anything, in fact, which displays a characteristic sort of activity which is not well-described by the sort of reductionistic analysis which chemists and physicists are sometimes tempted to offer. As non-material parts, these forms cannot in principle be explained in material terms; there is therefore no concern that these forms might disappear or be shown up as otiose upon further inspection. In fact they underwrite the possibility of inspection. When Legolas encounters the mallorn trees in Lothlórien and expresses his wish to "see now what is their shape and way of growth," he is talking about the mallorn trees. It would be no explanation at all for an atomist to explain that in fact the mallorn tree was at root no different from the orc, as both are just conglomerated atoms which don't differ much in their essentials. Legolas has as his object of study and admiration the mallorn tree, and if an explanation of the tree leaves out the tree, it has been shown thereby to be a bad explanation.

CHRISTIAN HYLOMORPHISM

The Aristotelian confidence in common sense long lay dormant in European philosophy, roughly from the sack of Rome and subsequent collapse of the Western Roman Empire in the fifth century to the re-introduction of Aristotle's texts (in Latin translations) into Europe starting in the twelfth century with the pioneering translations of James of Venice and completed in the thirteenth century, followed by additional translations by Gerard of Cremona and Michael Scot, who used Arabic versions of Aristotle, and by William of Moerbeke, who translated just about all of Aristotle from the original Greek. By the time Duns

Scotus arrived at Oxford, he would have had access to any Aristotelian text his heart desired. He wrote commentaries on several books of Aristotle, including *Metaphysics*, *On the Soul*, and several of the logical writings. Beyond the commentaries, his other writings display, on nearly every page, some debt to Aristotle.

One of these debts has to do with Duns Scotus's adoption of Aristotle's concept of form. The material that anything is made of, Scotus recognizes, has the capacity to become any other sort of thing. Matter is in flux, always "longing" to take on some new structure. Yet we perceive in nature various stable forms, not just oaks and dogs but flowers and people, rocks and water. Yes, these things are subject to change and ultimately decay. No material thing lasts forever, even diamonds, save by miraculous intervention. And these stable forms have stable patterns of change and growth. The matter which is caught up into the life of a dog behaves rather differently from the matter caught up into the life of an oak, and still more differently from the matter caught up in the explosion of fireworks. This stability in nature is not well explained by purely material processes, Scotus recognized, and so he followed Aristotle in postulating that additional principle, form, which does explain that stability, and that difference in structure and pattern of change which different kinds of things display.

This doctrine that material things are composites of matter and form is usually referred to nowadays as *hylomorphism*, a compound word taken from the Greek which simply means "matter/form-ism." In the great Scholastic age in which Scotus flourished hylomorphism was all the rage. It gave very powerful expression to the Christian idea that when God created the heavens and the earth and all the creatures therein, He really did create distinct kinds of things, with their own natures: birds of the air and fishes of the sea, beasts and creeping things and the strangest beasts of all, Adam and Eve. A theological embrace of various aspects of the theory of evolution poses no real threat to this scientific embrace of the creation myth of Genesis. True, evolution forces us not to take Creation as a six-day process, as we reckon days. But biblical commentators as far back as St. Augustine were already seeking understanding of their faith in the Genesis account of creation in non-literal ways. Modern empirical evidence that creation occurred over a much longer frame of time serves to support, not debunk, the witness of the Church Fathers. The Christian is free to worship God as the Creator however long the process turns out to be. In fact, the hylomorphic worldview is itself easily adaptable to the longer timeframe. No, we cannot agree with Aristotle that species of living things are fixed and immutable. The forms of things appear to be somewhat plastic. Taxonomists reckon that all the breeds of domestic dogs are equally members of just one species, *canis domesticus*. But any viewer of the Westminster Kennel Club Dog Show can witness the extraordinary range of that domesticated form. Exactly how the forms are to be enumerated and how they are to be distinguished is not really the job of the philosopher or theologian. The exact relationship between the form of *canis domesticus* and the forms of its various canine cousins is work for the biological systematician to do. The point here is just that the systematician has a subject matter to ponder precisely because physics and chemistry do not offer the final word about the things there really are. There are such things as forms, and because there are, physics and chemistry do not have the monopoly on scientific truth—and still less on philosophical and theological truth.

Busting up all claims to such a monopoly is important not just for scientists but for theologians too. Theology after all has a very special interest in that singular biological species *homo sapiens*. Theology has an exclusionary concern with this one species, even if it is not silent about its cladistic cousins. Christian theology obviously holds Man in high regard, regarding him as enjoying the highest degree of God's love for creatures. If there is no fundamental difference between the kind of thing we really are and the kind of thing an oak or a dog or a firework is, then God's special attention toward us makes little sense at all: it is a divine fixation with certain arbitrary regions of space and the particles which happen to occupy those regions. Even granting our unworthiness of this divine attention, we should at least extend God the credit of having loved, and died for, something rather more interesting than arbitrary collections of particles. And this is where we get the real theological payoff of the doctrine of hylomorphism: we human beings are a distinct and unique species among all the kinds of things that exist, and God loved us, became one of us, lived an exemplary human life to show us how to live, died for us, and rose again, giving us the extraordinary hope that we, alone among all animals, might live after death.

CHRISTOCENTRIC HYLOMORPHISM

In 1312 the Council of Vienne (France) defined that the human soul is the form of the body. The most plausible way of understanding this definition, in the context of its day, is that a human being is neither a mere soul trapped in a body nor a mere lump of matter careening through space but a composite of form and matter, where the form, because of its special status as the form of a human life, is a rational soul. As form, the rational soul structures matter and patterns its movements in the distinctively human way we recognize when we consider the lifetime of a human being. From this perspective, the human organism is one among many, though with the special status of chief of all animals. But as a rational soul, this form is what endows us with our distinctively human powers, intellect and will. It is because our souls are rational souls that we are *persons* and not mere beasts.

A metaphysical controversy arose in the thirteenth century over just how many forms a human being really has. From the outside, this controversy has all the markings of that classic example of a fruitless Scholastic question: how many angels can dance on the point of a pin? That particular disputation is not fruitless, however, because it helps us to think through the implications of how purely spiritual beings like angels might be able to interact with the material world. It helps us make some sense of the book of Revelation, for example, in which we read that around one single throne flew ten thousand times ten thousand angels. Surely the thought of one million rhinoceroses dancing around a single throne, not to mention the point of a pin, beggars belief. But angels are not like rhinoceroses: one million angels at a single point in space are a concentration of spiritual benevolence so powerful that no army can stand against it, and this is what Elisha and the servant saw when Aram rode out in force upon the Israelites (II Kings 6:17). That subtle Scholastic dispute focuses our attention on the way in which the goodness of God, channeled through his messengers, can hit full force at any and every point of space—a deployability even the Navy Seals would envy. How reassuring!

There is something comparably reassuring, if not so sublime, in that other subtle Scholastic controversy about how many forms a human being really has. This dispute centered on what became of the dead body of Christ, when Our Lord lay dead in the tomb. Whatever the harrowing of hell amounts to, that was the job of the soul of Christ. His body meanwhile lay in the tomb, and was as dead as Jacob Marley, dead as a doornail. During that most desperate time of human history, the body of Christ lay embalmed and shrouded in the tomb. After the heart-breaking but reverent work of spicing and shrouding the corpse, the holy women came to the tomb, if for no other reason than to venerate the body of their dead Lord. But that reverence, and that veneration, make little sense on the supposition that a human being has but a single form. Consider: the doctrine of hylomorphism tells us that the difference between this particular human being and some particular clump of particles is precisely that the human being is material bits formed by the rational soul. Take that soul away, and the matter left over is no different, in its basic constituents, from pond scum. Looked at in this way, it would seem foolish, if not weirdly animistic, to venerate the corpse of Christ. Without his form, there is nothing of Christ left over, just a Christ-resembling residue which gravity and rot have not yet succeeded in dissolving. Scotus and other Scholastics were repelled by this dishonorable thought, and so re-thought the whole framework of Aristotle's hylomorphism to accommodate the piety evident in the disciples' veneration of the body of Christ.

Scotus speculated that a human being has forms additional to the rational soul, forms which structure matter into that peculiar shape and organization of a human body and its human limbs and organs, bones and flesh. In most human deaths, a corpse remains. The natural way to think about these remains is that they are really continuous with the human being whose remains they are. The person has departed from us, but he has left something behind, something that was really him while he lived, though of course not the whole of him. Death really is the cessation of that person's presence among us, and the hylomorphist explains this cessation by saying that the rational soul no longer informs the body. In death, the soul has been separated, and its separated sojourn is a matter of pious speculation: purgatory for most of us (one hopes), heaven for some, and for Christ, harrowing hell. But, barring catastrophic deaths by, for example, incineration, there is no need to speculate about the body's earthly sojourn: here it is in the morgue, the church, the crypt, the cemetery. The veneration we owe the dead makes more sense on the supposition that this very body now dead was the very body of our dearly departed. Scotus's theorizing gave intellectual heft to this habit of honoring corpses. He proposed that a human being is a composite of matter and more than one form: one of these forms is the rational soul, and it is the seat of those powers because of which a living person really is living and really is a person. But that person is also a body, of a particular shape and organization, and these typically remain after death. The matter left over, so shaped and so arranged, is not like pond scum. It bears still the integrity of a human body, an integrity powerfully expressed, to choose a favorite from a wealth of examples, in Peter Paul Rubens's *Entombment*. And to Bl. John's pious philosophical imagination, the only way to account for the likeness of the corpse to the man, and the propriety of venerating the corpse, was to suppose that that corpse too had at least one form which was there all along during the life of Christ. The loss of Christ's soul is sufficient for Christ really to be dead; but the presence of the form or forms of the body of Christ is sufficient for Christ's dead body really to be Christ's, and so really to be honored.

Scotus also extended the honor of having multiple forms to all human beings. But the wellspring of this generous theory of forms was his reflection on Christ in the tomb. This Christocentric method characterized much of Scotus's speculative work, but it has a special poignancy where it was applied to the dead (and soon to be risen) Christ. Christ is as human as he is God, so in learning what must be said of Christ as human we learn what must be said of all humans, as humans. God the Son assumed humanity, not pond scum. So his ongoing union with the corpse of Christ, in those three days in the tomb, is sufficient to show that he continued to be united with something human, not scummy. This is all that is needed to infer that all other human beings also have this multi-form structure. As a human, Christ is not some special case. What makes him different from us is his divinity. So if it must be maintained that Christ has more than one form, then it must be maintained that all humans do too. It is a funny thing about us that it is practically impossible to feel the importance of having more than one form, considering ourselves in the abstract. But in bereavement, when you are inclined by piety and common sense to believe that it is something of your loved one there on the bed, or in the coffin, then the existential value of Scotus's theory begins to emerge.

There is yet more existential value to his theory of many forms, though here we run the risk of splitting hairs, or hearts. It is the long custom of the Church to venerate not just whole bodies of holy people, but their body parts. The heart of St. John Vianney, for example, the heart of that holy priest who died in 1859, remains incorrupt to this day. It is rightly venerated as the bodily organ which pumped the blood of a saint, and the symbolic organ of a life on fire for the care of souls. Scotus's many-formed theory of the hylomorphic structure of a human being gives us good reason to think that that heart is the very heart of that saint while he lived. It is not a mere residue, having no meaningful continuity with the bodily life of St. John. It is in truth his very heart. Veneration of first-class relics is impoverished if we do not follow Scotus in supposing that not just the bodies but even the body parts of human beings may have their own distinctive forms. The whole human being is still a unity, all the distinctly formed parts united together into a single life by the one form which is the rational soul. But under the unifying and organizational work of the rational soul are a thousand genuine body parts, equally parts of the living man as the soul, yet not, of course, as important as the soul. If, *per impossibile*, we had the very soul of St. John Vianney among us, we would simply ignore his heart; but if the heart is all we have left, our piety is not in vain if we extend to it something of the honor we would extend to the saint himself.

THE VINDICATION OF REALISM

By now I hope you have seen how Scotus's adoption of Aristotle's hylomorphism is a philosophical expression of St. Francis's song of all creation. It leaves intact the individual members of the chorus of creation, each having its own part. In this sense the doctrine of form is a celebration of diversity: the world really is divided into different kinds of things, each with its own distinctive voice. Whatever their material commonality, an oak is not a dog is not a human, because these three have different kinds of forms. But now I would like to explore the unity amid all this diversity, focusing on the specific sort of unity shared by individual members of one single kind. Some in the Middle Ages, and many today, deny that there really is any such unity. This negative view, known as *nominalism*, holds that our concepts of kinds of things—for example, the kind human being—correspond to no real unity among things such as humans. The unity among the humans is all of our own making, words or concepts made up for the convenience of identifying some similar things with just one word or concept. (The word "nominalism" itself comes from the Latin *nomen*, meaning *name*.) Scotus emphatically affirmed the very opposite of nominalism. The opposite of nominalism goes by the name *realism*, and realism holds that members of a single kind, such as all the humans, really are united in their humanity. They *share* humanity. No one has all of it to himself. And there are not different humanities, one for each human. There is one humanity. Each human being, no matter what race, or class, or sex, or level of ability, has the same human nature. No matter who we are, we are the same: human.

The debate between nominalists and realists arises from some very commonplace observations. Consider two human beings, John and Thomas. They really are two. But they are both human. We group them together under a single kind, human. And we are right to do so. As far their humanity goes, there is nothing to tell them apart. So they are two things but have one nature. This is a classic example of what philosophers sometimes call *the problem of the One and the Many*. The many humans seem to be unified—literally, *as one*—so how do we explain this oneness in multitude? The nominalist says that their oneness is due merely to the way that we think or speak—they are one only in name; whereas the realist says that their oneness is on the side of reality: there really is something they share in common, humanity.

The advantage of realism over nominalism may be seen in a very practical way by considering the study and practice of medicine. Medical students study textbooks which have lots of words about human physiology, and lots of illustrations of particular human bodies. These students also study cadavers. Their teachers, wise realists as they are in practice, whatever their professed philosophy, assume that if their students learn all about these illustrations and cadavers, they thereby gain the sort of knowledge they need to practice medicine on *all the humans*. The few examples they study in medical school are supposed to stand in for all the humans. And they do. This is because all the humans are sufficiently united in their forms of life that by learning in intimate detail how one or two work, the medical student learns how they all work.

The nominalist of course will not deny the phenomenon of the phenomenal success of medical science. But on his worldview the phenomenon is miraculous, or at least mere coincidence. In reality all the humans share nothing in common, so how comes it that by studying one, medical students gain insight into the many? The basic nominalist answer is that there is a bunch of individual things that just happen to be similar to each other, and this similarity is what undergirds the transferability of medical knowledge from the one to the many. But this sort of answer does not explain away the miracle, or coincidence, of the phenomenon: it simply embraces it as miraculous or coincidental.

The realist does not rest content with the nominalist answer. For the realist, there is one human nature, and all the human beings share it. Medical students gain knowledge of the many through the one because the one has the same nature as the many. There is no miracle or coincidence here: it is the structure of reality as God has made it that things come in kinds, and belonging to a kind is a matter of sharing something in common.

But if the realist eschews miracle and coincidence as an explanation of the phenomenon of unity in diversity, he still has explanatory work of his own to do. One thing to note is that the unity of a natural kind like humanity is somewhat different from more homespun unities. Human nature is not the sort of thing which is spread out across all the humans, like a blanket. When my family and I share one blanket while snuggling on the couch to watch a movie, each of us has just a part of the blanket, and somehow Dad always ends up with a small part. But our shared humanity is not like this. Each human is fully human, having all there is to have in being human. Co-blanketed people by contrast don't have all the blanket they share, even if the lucky small ones might be fully blanketed by their generous portion of the blanket.

Yet while a human being does indeed have all there is to have in being human, we obviously don't mean to imply that there is but one human, one super-organism, like the Borg Collective, in which individual humanoids are really just parts of one organism. The way humanity is shared by all humans is not that way. You are one human with the whole of human nature, and I am one, too. So humanity is not shared by each human having a different part of it, nor is it shared by there being just one human. We might say that humanity is a *shareable but indivisible unity*. Shareable, like the blanket; indivisible, like the Borg Collective. But both shareable and indivisible, and so different from either of these. Scotus's own expression for this sort of unity is *less than numerical unity*.

The less than numerical unity of our shared human nature matters a great deal not just for metaphysics, but for ethics and politics. All the humans have human nature equally, and fully, and therefore, insofar as being human is what matters for ethics and politics, any human being is someone we are called to love as our neighbor and to ensure is included in political life in such a way that he or she enjoys all the benefits of living in a just and civilized society. It is on the basis of the metaphysical commitment to realism that we can rationally condemn all past and current efforts to degrade our fellow human beings, including the disabled, the sick, the elderly, the unborn, and those of ethnicities different from our own. And this is why Scotus's realism, no less than his hylomorphism, is such a fitting philosophical flowering of the Franciscan movement: for Francis showed us, as well as any saint in the history of the Church, what it means to love every human being as a member of the family.

6

YOU ARE UNIQUE

> His Divine Majesty foresaw you in His sovereign goodness and loved you exceedingly. When did He begin to love you? When He began to be God. And when was His beginning? Never, for He has always been, without beginning and without end: wherefore He has always loved you, and from eternity prepared the favors and graces which he has bestowed upon you.
>
> —St. Francis de Sales, *An Introduction to the Devout Life*

> [One] important facet of Franciscan spirituality was its intense focus on the person of Jesus Christ. This devotion . . . ends up giving a new status to the particular, as something more than a mere instantiation of the universal. . . . With hindsight we can recognize this as a major turning point in Western civilization, an important step towards that primacy of the individual which defines our culture. But of course, it could only have this significance because it was more than a mere intellectual shift. . . . It was primarily a revolution in devotion, in the focus of prayer and love: the paradigm human individual, the God-Man.
>
> —Charles Taylor, *A Secular Age*

THE POLITICS OF INDIVIDUALITY

The whole human family is united in its humanity. Our humanity, we might say, is that which makes us all the same. It is in respect of other things, things besides our humanity, that we are different. The differences are to be celebrated, not resisted, unless they involve injustice. Many of these differences draw people together in ways that are very meaningful for them: the difference of sex which divides but draws together man and woman; the difference of kinship relations which draw people together into families through the unique dependencies, sacrifices, and intimacy of family life; the difference of culture by which many individual families are one community through their shared values, experiences, and stories; and so on. These sorts of ties bind some people together while excluding other people, and these various forms of difference are one source of conflict and violence among men. But the violence which these intimate ties often inspire is no reason to be suspicious of either difference itself or the exclusion which difference demands. We human beings quite literally need some forms of exclusion, since our gestation in the womb is long, and our helpless youth is longer. Having a child in my care makes it obvious that this tiny person deserves a greater portion of my care than other people, and this tiny person deserves to be protected from external threats. That extra measure of care and that readiness to protect are the twin foundations of the exclusionary society. If one understands what it's like to have babies around, then being on the outside of some exclusionary circle is nothing to be concerned about, since one understands and respects that need to provide and protect, and one is meeting that need in one's own little exclusionary society. As discrete units, however, these little societies support and enrich one another: individuals form the family, families form cultures and nations, nations make trade agreements and treaties, and we're all better off for it than if the one human family were compelled to endure central planning from some unelected multinational nanny-dictatorship.

It shouldn't need to be said, but it does, that difference and hence exclusion are also requirements for true diversity. Where exclusion is impermissible there can be no local flavor: no special customs or dialects or aesthetic ideals; nothing private or peculiar or eccentric; no inside jokes. Familiar strips of big-box chain stores surrounded by acres of asphalt give us a very good idea of the bland homogeneity of a world in which exclusion and therefore diversity have been eradicated.

Important as these various differences are to any individual's self-understanding, they do not make her the very individual she is. To be the sort of thing that can belong to a time and a place and a people, she must already be an individual. Before she is a daughter or a sister or a citizen, she is a human being. But simply being human is clearly not sufficient to make her the very individual she is, because being human is what all humans have in common. We recognize that she must have an identity which is prior to her situation in a nexus of social relations, but her humanity cannot explain that priority.

Suppose that there is nothing after all which makes her a unique, irreplaceable person whose role in the social nexus she inhabits is like a character in a novel. Perhaps her identity is more like a cog, with identical copies producible on a mass scale, and her role in the social nexus more like a machine in which that cog—or any other just like it—plays some functional role. It might be thought that realism lends itself to the cog-in-the-machine approach to a human being's relationship to herself and the social world. It says after all that what we are, at the fundamental level, are human beings—and therefore at the fundamental level we are all the same.

Bl. John's own version of realism, properly understood, is impervious to this sort of abuse, because it postulates some principle, additional to our humanity, responsible not for making us the kind of thing we are, but for making us the very individual each of us is. Scotus's realism, fully ramified, therefore strikes a blow for the uniqueness and irreplaceability of every human being. The philosopher Charles Taylor, in his justly celebrated intellectual history *A Secular Age*, asserts that the Franciscan movement in general and Scotus in particular are pivotal in the history of Western civilization as harbingers of a "turn to the individual," in which the individual person takes on an unprecedented level of significance in philosophy, theology, spirituality, ethics, and politics. According to Taylor, Scotus's importance in this turn to the individual lies in his intricate metaphysical explanation of what precisely makes two human beings different from each other. Scotus in fact was the first philosopher in the history of Western thought to advance a realist theory of the individual which made the individual truly unique. This is because Scotus was the first to theorize that each individual had its own individualizing feature, a feature that could not in principle be shared with any other thing. In the philosophical lore, this individualizing entity has come to be called *thisness*, or, adapting the Latin, *haecceity* (usually pronounced *hayx-ee-i-tee*). So while all human beings are the same insofar as they are human, each has its own haecceity and is therefore a unique instance of a human being: you are unique.

Given his focus on individuals, Scotus is sometimes accused of being a nominalist or proto-nominalist. From the previous chapter it should be evident that these charges could only be made in ignorance of what Scotus actually thinks. To think that Scotus's focus on individuals puts him somehow on the side of the nominalists is about as reasonable as thinking that Richard Dawkins is a theologian because he has written some things about God. The fact is that Scotus developed his own doctrine of the uniqueness of each individual in exactly the same context as his realist theory of universal natures. So in Scotus's own exposition, the precise sense in which we all share human nature and the precise sense in which each of us is an individual human are inextricably related. If our humanity makes us all the same, what makes us different? Again, it can't be our humanity itself that makes each of us the very individual each of us is—because our humanity is the very thing which unites us with all other humans. One of the great intellectual controversies of the Middle Ages focused precisely on this question: what is the principle of individuation? Scotus's answer to this question was simultaneously the most thorough and the most original ever offered in this long medieval debate.

This unique haecceity that each of us has is fully known only to God. Scotus speculates that in heaven God might grant us a special insight into the unique haecceity of each person. For now, we know it only as that entity which secures the unique individuality of each person. Politically speaking, this doctrine of individuality means that we are not interchangeably human, to be counted as "human resources" or "manpower," or herded into communes and worked as tools for a Great Leap Forward. Our uniqueness should also make us wary of the strange modern obsession with counting human beings, turning them into statistics about human populations, statistics wielded in fights for political power or waved in warnings about population booms or busts—as if the fact that we're all human made us collectively the sort of things of which there could be too many or too few. Maybe God was on to something when he became angry at King David for conducting a census (II Sam 24:10).

THE METAPHYSICS OF INDIVIDUALITY

Valuable as it is to reckon ourselves members of a common human family, it is equally valuable to recognize our unrepeatable individuality. To get a sense of the originality of Scotus's theory of haecceity, it is helpful to consider some of the alternative views kicked around in the lecture halls of Oxford and Paris in his day. Here's a plausible first alternative. Grant that two human beings are the same insofar as they are human. But they differ in so many other ways: sex, height, weight, skin color, hair color, eye color, personality, hobbies, occupation, and so on. Surely no two people in the world match up in all these features. If not, then we could say that while our human nature unites us, our distinctive sets of characteristics differentiate us.

Scotus is ready with criticism of this easy alternative. Each of the characteristics just mentioned, sex, height, weight, and so on, is in principle shareable. If one person can weigh two hundred pounds, then two people can too. Same for being six feet tall, male, blue-eyed, and so on. It is of the nature of these and like features to be shareable. Now consider this: not only are individual features like these shareable, but so are combinations of features like these. If one person can both weigh two hundred pounds and have blue eyes, then another person can have just this duet of features, too. And we can build up from here. Imagine some extraordinarily long and detailed description of a person; however nuanced the description, however eccentric the person described, that long description could conceivably fit someone else equally well. Imagine listing all the qualities you love about your beloved; not only might any one of them belong to someone else as well, but all of them together might belong to someone else as well. Yet you love one person, not two.

So where does this leave us? One initially sensible suggestion is that two or more things are distinct not because of their characteristics (for all the reasons just given), but because they are made up of different material parts. Fine, you might say, I see how all my characteristics might be shared with another person, but I am I and he is he because I'm made of this stuff and he's made of that stuff. Maybe our matter distinguishes us.

Definitely not, says Scotus. If your matter makes you an individual, then it follows that wherever your matter is there you are, too. But this can't be right, because eventually you'll die, and when you die that matter you were made of will go on existing. We might be forced to say that when you die you *become* soil, then grass, then cow, then dinner; but we don't want to say that you *are* soil, then you *are* grass, then you *are* cow, and then you *are* dinner. When we say you become these things we imply that you (or perhaps just your body) cease to exist and something else, the soil, then the grass, etc., comes into existence. But if matter makes you an individual, then we're forced to say against our better judgment that you go on existing through all these different forms. Another way to put the objection is this: you cannot be a cow, but the matter you're made of can be the matter of a cow (it is, Scotus says, *indifferent* to being a cow or a steak or an oak tree or a scorpion), so your matter cannot be what makes you you.

If not your characteristics or your matter, what other options do we have? Scotus addresses a few other, rather abstruse, theories about what makes you an individual, but these need not detain us. My students sometimes suggest a theory that Scotus himself did not explicitly evaluate. They say that perhaps what makes you an individual is your soul. They understand that your matter can be anyone else's and therefore can't do the trick, and they understand that your characteristics can be shared by many things at once and therefore can't do the trick, so they suggest that your soul can secure your uniqueness. It's not an obviously false theory, but it can't be right by Scotus's lights. First, when Scotus asks what it is that makes an individual thing to be individual, he is thinking more broadly than just individual humans. He has in mind any individual whatsoever, including humans, other living things, and non-living things. Second, for Scotus a human soul is not just some generic mind or spirit, but the specific form of human life. Your soul is not only what makes you a thinking thing, but a living thing; and not just any living thing but a human being. All humans therefore share the same kind of soul, so your soul isn't what captures the difference between your being human and your being you. Besides, and third and finally, saying that your soul is what makes you unique is just to back up the question. We're left with a new question: what makes your soul unique, given that it is the same in kind as every other human soul? So with all due respect to my students, their theory will not work.

Scotus concludes that every individual has some totally unique, impossible-to-repeat, individualizing aspect, a haecceity. Scotus's thought here is that since your essence—humanity, if you are who I think you are—cannot make you unique because all human beings have humanity in common, and since your characteristics cannot make you unique because they too are shared or are shareable by many things, and since your matter cannot make you unique because your matter can take on any number of different forms that you cannot take on, there must be something else, of an altogether different sort, that is in principle not shareable. It is what distinguishes you from all other things, it is what makes you not just a human being but this very human being. And more generally, he thinks that every individual, no matter its kind—individual dogs, individual oak trees—is made to be individual by a non-repeatable individuating entity.

We are again in deep philosophical waters, but we need to dive even deeper and make a couple clarifications, to avoid misunderstanding. First, your haecceity is not quite what makes you *you*. Instead, it is what makes you an *individual*. *You* are an individual human being, and an individual human being is a human nature made individual by a haecceity. This is crucial to keep in mind. Scotus does not think it possible that *you* might have been some other kind of thing. Of course, you might never have existed; you might have turned out to be a person with very different beliefs and a very different character from what you now have; but you, if you exist, exist as a human being, and this couldn't have been otherwise.

The second clarification is rather trickier. "Haecceity" is a word we use to name many things—any haecceity, in fact. But more exact language would use something like proper names to talk about the haecceities of different individuals. If I am Ward, we might call my haecceity my *Wardness*; your haecceity, Dear Reader, I would call your *Dear Readerness*, but that obviously wouldn't do, since that name wouldn't distinguish you from other Dear Readers (if we ever meet I would be happy to learn a better name for your haecceity). So while there are many things that have a haecceity, there is exactly one, and can be no more than exactly one, *Wardness*. Some dear readers might quibble that after all there are, and have been, and will be, many Wards (I can think of a few off the top of my head, actually), so aren't there in fact many *Wardnesses*? Well, yes. But just think about how proper names work. Even though you might say "Ward" to name any number of people, or even things (a psychiatric ward, a Mormon place of worship, etc.), when you call me "Ward" you mean to be referring to me, myself, this individual author of this book, irrespective of all the many things I have in common with many other individuals, and irrespective of all the other things called *Ward*. So, similarly, when you talk about my *Wardness* you're talking about my own haecceity and nothing else's, notwithstanding the fact that any other Ward you know has its own *Wardness*. A most exact language would have a unique word for every single haecceity. But we cannot speak so exactly.

GOD'S IDEA OF YOU

The gist of the last paragraph is that we cannot help *speaking* in generalities, even when grammatically general *words* get in the way of describing things as they are in themselves. God, blessed be He, does not have this problem. God has ideas not only of every actual thing but also of every possible thing. So He has ideas not only of humanity but of *Dear Readerness* and *Wardness*. When He thinks of you, He knows that thing that makes you unique, and He knows it intimately. According to Scotus, this is yet another way in which God's thoughts are not like our own.

We can only think about haecceity in a general way, as a theoretical entity posited to explain the phenomenon of individuality. Your uniqueness, at least in this life, is hidden from us, behind all those general characteristics that might help us to pick you out in a lineup of suspects but do not explain your individuality. God, on the other hand, knows your haecceity exactly as it is. His decision to create you, then, is not a decision to create a human being at such and such a time, in such and such a place, with such and such genetic information, having a proclivity for reading books on Duns Scotus, and so on, but a decision to create *you*, this thing he has been thinking for all eternity. God's eternal idea of your haecceity is Scotus's philosophical riff on Christ's assurance to us that God knows every sparrow and numbers every hair on our heads (Luke 12:7), or God's word to Jeremiah that before the prophet was born, or even formed in the womb, God knew him (Jer 1:5).

God's concern for every individual (and, according to the Gospel, for every *part* of every individual!) derives ultimately from the fact that God's unconstrained decision to create this world was in part a decision to create *you*. You and even your hairs were among God's reasons for making this world. God does nothing by accident or thoughtlessly; the world is ordered by love. And God is, as Scotus says, a most methodical lover; so when He wills the world He wills all its individuals.

I'D LOVE YOU ANYWAY

Scotus is clear that while God knows all haecceities, we earthly pilgrims do not know them. We never see through the cloak of generality, except in the very generic sense that we can come to know that every individual has its own individuating entity by reflecting on the philosophical problem of what makes a thing an individual. However well we get to know one another, Scotus thinks, we are always stuck with the generalities. Maybe in heaven we will have direct knowledge of haecceities, but not now. The reason is that we know individuals exclusively through our senses, and the only sort of information our senses gather is information that is shareable by many things. Scotus was unusual in his day for allowing the possibility that we can know an individual object without abstracting the common nature from its individuated condition—what he called *intuitive cognition*—but even this abstraction-free sort of knowing does not grant us direct cognitive access to haecceity; it merely grants the possibility that we can directly access an *individual*, which has a common essential nature, together with many common accidental natures (such as a color, a shape, a size, and so on) made individual *through* haecceity. But we do not know the haecceity itself.

On strict principles of metaphysics it is hard to argue with Scotus's contention that we can't naturally know these haecceities. But our experience of personal relationships with other people yields a different sort of data to be reckoned with, and I wonder whether Scotus should not have left open the possibility that we can after all come to know something about the inmost individuating feature of at least some individuals. I am in no position to offer a demonstration of this thesis, but I shall try to make it plausible.

Let's go back to the original statement of the philosophical issues that motivate Scotus's theory of individualization. The problem, recall, is that general characteristics can be shared by many things, and combinations of general characteristics can be shared by many things, so for any individual with any combination of general characteristics, however unusual and conspicuous, that combination is in principle shareable and therefore cannot be what makes that individual an individual.

I remember as a teenager going to a "purity talk" at a youth group meeting at church. These purity talks were all about dating and marriage and sex, and the basic advice we all received from these talks was basically right and pretty helpful; I'm grateful I got to hear them, even if there were some cringeworthy occasions. On the most cringeworthy occasion I can remember, we heard from a youngish married couple—they were about thirty, I think—who talked to us about how they met, how they behaved after they fell in love, how they decided it was the right time to marry, and so on. This was all rather sweet. Then they told us how, prior to meeting each other, each had drawn up a list of qualities they wanted in a spouse. The lists, they said, were very long and detailed. On the lists were physical features, character traits, vocational goals, hobbies, and on and on, and these lists were to function as a set of criteria by which to judge real, live, potential mates. They knew what they wanted, and they weren't going to let attractive people they actually knew deter them from getting what they wanted.

Then one day they met. He fell in love with her and, if I recall, she matched his list. She began to fall in love with him but, at first, she felt guilty for doing so because he lacked one crucial quality from her list. He was perfect in every other respect, she thought, but he did not make the cut; he fell short of the dreamed-up man who existed in her mind and on the sacred sheet of wide-ruled paper. What was this flaw, you ask? He was morally upright, he had all the right religious and political views, he was handsome enough and smart enough, but—he didn't like to ski. In fact he didn't know how to ski. He had never gone skiing. He enjoyed mountain-biking, which is seasonally incompatible with skiing. All her young life she had dreamed of skiing with her fantasy husband, and here was this attractive man on a bike. Since she believed her list to have been inspired by God's voice, she was genuinely concerned about staying in a relationship with this mountain-biker, fearing she might be disobeying God. Eventually, somehow, she figured out a way to be with this real man and not feel guilty, and apparently they've lived happily ever after.

You might infer from this vignette that the couple went on to advise us not to make lists, because you don't know what surprises life will bring you and you don't want to hem yourself into a self-made fantasy land. But no. This is not what they advised. Make your lists, they said; pray over your lists; pray for the man or woman out there waiting for you. But just be a little flexible so that if the almost-man-of-your-dreams turns out to have a driving passion to be a neurologist and not an endocrinologist, you'll not pass up the chance for wedded bliss.

There are several problems with the idea of a checklist of necessary qualifications for a potential spouse, but there's one problem we'll focus on here. This problem is that no list of qualities, however detailed, can ever be a description of what makes a person to be the very individual he or she is. Yes, it may turn out that there is one and only one person who satisfies all the list's criteria, and maybe miraculously you'll meet her! But in knowing all these qualities you do not know the person, because these qualities might have all been attached to a different person. So if this combination of qualities is what you love, then you simply do not love a person, for qualities do not a person make.

But we do love people, or at least some of us do. And while it's true that any of us lovers could list some of the qualities we love about those whom we love, few if any of us would say that any list of qualities we might draw up *exhausts* what we love about the person. There always remains the non-qualitative fact that she is herself, he is himself. To see this, think of the way people change as they age, both in mind and in body. Bodies grow old; and while an older body is not unqualifiedly less beautiful than a young body, it's undeniable that the special beauty of a youthful body does not remain in one's spouse of twenty years. Minds age, too. The hope for us all is that our minds become more beautiful as our bodies grow less beautiful—a consolation in our old age—but this does not happen in every respect for everyone. One gets older and, let's say, becomes less selfish, more patient, capable of a greater love; but one also grows careworn, wounded by loss, slower to rejoice. In any case, whatever qualities of mind one loved in the beloved twenty years ago, they have not endured all together to the present. If all that was loved at the start were those qualities, then we'd have to infer that love ceases when those qualities changed. But in successful marriages this is just not true. Nor is it true to say that over twenty years one loves a succession of sets of qualities. No, it is the person who is loved, the very person who now has these qualities and will come eventually to have different qualities. As the great Randy Travis sings, "They say time takes its toll on a body, / Makes a young girl's brown hair turn gray. / Honey, I don't care, I ain't in love with your hair / And if it all fell out, well I'd love you anyway." Because qualities are shareable and because the qualities of any one person change over time, it seems reasonable to think that, in love, the lover gains some sort of access to the person, to the bearer of those qualities.

So in the end I'm not convinced that Bl. John is right to deny that we can have some access to that positive entity that makes a thing the very individual it is. I think we *experience* some things around us, perhaps exclusively other people with whom we enjoy close relationships, in their individuality. But this quibble with Scotus should not obscure the real point of this chapter, which was to reflect on Scotus's reasons for thinking that each one of us, and each individual thing, has some special individualizing facet that sets us apart from every other individual and makes us to be the very individuals we are. Your haecceity is known by God, and his choice to make this world is in part a choice to make you—not merely a human being with all your qualities, but you.

7

PURPOSES NATURAL AND DIVINE

But it is precisely that for the love of which the efficient cause brings something to be that, as loved, is the final cause of what was made, for it was to the beloved that the latter is ordered.... At times, it may well be that the object of the ultimate operation is something loved ... and therefore it would be the final cause. But it would not be because it is the term of such a nature's operation, but rather because it is loved by that which causes this nature. Nevertheless, it is not without reason that the ultimate operation of a thing or the object attained thereby is at times referred to as an end, for it is ultimate and is in some way the best and as such verifies some of the requirements for a final cause.

—Bl. John Duns Scotus, *A Treatise on the First Principle*

God can be posited as the immediate end of anything whatsoever. This [object, i.e. God] as it exists in itself is the end and is loved. Everything else, whether it be an operation or an object, is not an end in an unqualified sense, but only with respect to His liberality.

—Bl. John Duns Scotus, *Questions on the* Metaphysics *of Aristotle*

Shall I tell you the secret of the whole world? It is that we have only known the back of the world. We see everything from behind, and it looks brutal. That is not a tree, but the back of a tree. That is not a cloud, but the back of a cloud. Cannot you see that everything is stooping and hiding a face? If we could only get round in front.

—G. K. Chesterton, *The Man Who Was Thursday*

PHILOSOPHERS EXIST

By the way, you really do exist. If it seems philosophically trivial to assert that you exist, it is worth considering a rival philosophy touted by some of our celebrated scientists and philosophers—a philosophy which is a rival to Scotus's in the sense that it denies that you exist. To their way of thinking, modern physics has revealed the world to be incompatible with such a thing as consciousness. If they are right, then our own consciousness is just an illusion. But if this is true, then the basic entities postulated by modern physics have the very peculiar power that they can produce, in us, the illusion of consciousness. Let that fanciful thought sink into your consciousness. Despite the fact that these physical bits are supposed to be the only things there are, they can produce in *us*—things like authors and readers of books about the philosophical implications of physics—illusions of having consciousness. One wonders what the difference between consciousness and an illusion of consciousness might be.

Descartes and St. Augustine are the well-known guides for helping us see that there is no difference, but Scotus too thought that we have immediate awareness of, and certitude about, at least some of the contents of our own minds. Famously, Descartes tried to express serious worries that he might be deceived about everything he believed. St. Augustine long before him reflected on what logically follows from the proposition that I am wrong about everything I believe. Both realized, in different ways, that it is incoherent to assert a view of the world in which things like philosophers don't exist. Even if I am deceived in as comprehensive a way as possible, I cannot be deceived about this: whether my thinking is correct or incorrect, I am thinking, and so I at least exist. A contradiction follows from the proposition that I am wrong about everything I think, because the proposition entails both that I do not think, since I believe that I think, and that I do think, since I must be thinking in order to be wrong in my thinking. But if a proposition entails a contradiction then we know it is false. Hence it is simply not true that I am wrong about everything I believe.

What must be true about the world if there are to be things like illusions in it? I don't think elementary particles have illusions, however unpredictably they might behave. Nor do I think that diamonds or roses or cockroaches have illusions. In fact, the great misfortune of having an illusion can only befall things which are conscious; there can be no illusions in a world without consciousness. Therefore to assert that there is such a thing as an illusion of consciousness entails a contradiction: that there is no consciousness, since it is an illusion, and that there is consciousness, since there are illusions. Descartes and Augustine might say that if I have an illusion, then I am conscious. And if I am conscious, then consciousness exists, and I exist, and therefore the elementary particles are not the only things which exist. The problem with philosophers who pay too much heed to physics is that they often forget there are such things as physicists and philosophers. This is where the classical and medieval philosophy of form supplies the needed link between the physicist's description of the world and the ordinary person's assurance that there are indeed such things as people, too.

The human being, considered as a rational investigator of its world, is a material thing, but it is a material thing under a certain form, what Scotus and others called the rational soul. The composite unity of form and matter, the human being, is endowed with certain powers which literally stretch beyond the powers native to its basic material constituents. We stretch beyond our material boundaries whenever we perceive the things around us, and that includes the books in which we read assertions about how we do not exist after all. Our eyes and ears and so on are passive in the sense that when they come into contact with light, or food, things simply happen to them. They swoon before the sensory world, but they are not helpless. Their passivity initiates the complicated chain of physical reactions which mysteriously gives rise to the experience of seeing and tasting. And these experiences in turn are part of the process by which we are able to form concepts of the things that give rise to them. These concepts in turn are what equip us to think about things not simply as stimuli to our sensory organs but as things in themselves, things with their own peculiar forms and habits, pursuing their own ends, apart from us and yet available to us as things to be observed, studied, used, and admired. We are thinking animals, and this means we can do more than navigate the world more or less successfully in response to stimuli. We can understand the world, and the things in it. And we can make some reasonable guesses about how things are out there.

WHOSE PURPOSES?

Our own experience of seeking understanding clues us into the way things work in the world at large. We ourselves have cognitive powers whose natural goal is understanding. Understanding is among those things that peculiar power of mind is for. Even when our range of interests is rather limited, we seek to figure things out. And even when most of our seeking is for the sake of fulfilling some very practical need, nearly all of us recognize that there are times when we simply want to understand, for the joy of it. Understanding, therefore, is among the goals of our thinking. And in this sense the activity of thinking is therefore purposeful. In our own lives, then, we can detect the reality of purposeful activity, and so know that purposeful activity is among the phenomena of the natural world, insofar as we are part of the natural world.

I do not say that the purposefulness of our own intellectual activity is how we first come to know that the natural world includes purposeful activity. Far from it, in fact. It is much more common for kids to begin to understand the purposefulness of nature by learning about plants and animals, in school or, ideally, by having the luxury to sit around outside and watch the world go by. But there is strategic value to having the purposes of our own minds as a back-up example of the purposefulness of nature. Should we come to doubt the purposefulness of nature, at the least we can have our own purposefulness to safeguard our sanity.

Why do birds fly south during winter? Why do bears hibernate? Why do snakes shed their skin? Why do squirrels gather nuts? Why do bees dance? It's because these activities—migrating, hibernating, and so on—have an undeniable purpose. The birds fly south in order to maintain their supply of food; the bears hibernate in order to conserve energy; and so on. These simple cases are paradigmatic of what philosophers call a "teleological" conception of the natural world, from the Greek words *telos* (end, goal) and *logos* (reason, study). On the teleological conception, all or most of what happens in the world happens for some purpose.

We could say, "happens for some reason," but this wouldn't be quite innocent. "Happening for a reason" has a distinctively theological ring to it, doesn't it? It might put us in mind of what St. Paul says in Romans: "all things work together for the good. . . ." People sometimes say, "Everything happens for a reason," when they're trying to offer consolation, implying that there's some "higher power" overseeing the cosmos. Religious people tend to be totally comfortable with this theological teleology, but it's important to keep in mind that it's possible to think that the natural world is teleological while denying that God exists or that God is interested in what goes on in the natural world. Indeed, whatever your theological or religious beliefs, you're bound to think that there is some purpose to what the birds and bees are doing.

Yes, but are you bound to think this because it's obvious and true, or are you bound to think it out of habit and custom, the way that we all think of the sun *rising* in the morning and *setting* in the evening? In other words, does your commonsense belief about nature's purposes amount to *insight* about how the world works, or is it something more like a *projection* of your human point of view onto the natural world? Many scientists and philosophers reject the teleological conception of nature as just such a projection of the human point of view. We often have purposes in our own actions and we know what it's like to act with a goal in mind. We're so accustomed to thinking this way that we just assume that other things also act for goals. But we also assume, the teleology deniers will point out, that these other things do not have minds for goals to be in. How then, they will ask, can these other things really have purposes to their actions?

Historically, there have been two ways of answering the question. The first is simply to give up your belief in nature's purposes. The second is to come up with some version of teleology that doesn't have the very interesting but sadly untrue implication that everything has a mind. If you take the second way, either your version of teleology will have something to do with God or it won't. The main problem with a godless teleology is not strictly speaking that purposeful action as such is unintelligible without God. Instead the problem is that there wouldn't be anything without God, and so there wouldn't be any purposes without God. So if we are stuck with God, it is a good thing to wonder what He might have to do with teleology. Now one sort of view about what God has to do with teleology is that God bestows purposes on things. Here are the things God has made, and there are some purposes, and without God none of the purposes would be assigned to any of the things.

Now the view that God is the mind at the back of all purpose, or at least all purposeful actions performed by things which themselves lack minds, might seem nice and comforting; we might form some idea of God benevolently ordering things so that they come out well, in a sense that perfectly matches how we prefer or expect things to be. But there is something unsettling about the thought that the natural world has its purposes only because God has intervened by giving it purposes which it would otherwise lack. This thought holds that things without minds have their purposes given to them by God. Without God's correlation of *this* purpose with *that* action, we'd have to say that that action is purposeless. If this is how things are, then it is hard to see how we could know that He assigns just the purposes to natural things which we assign to them when we observe them.

Look around you. See the spider spinning her web and the birds gathering twigs; see the sea turtles going ashore and the dolphin surfacing. You can't help but form ideas about the purposes of all these actions. But the thought of a free God assigning purposes to natural things should give you pause. What connection is there between the action—going ashore—and the thing you think is the purpose of the action—laying eggs? Sure, the second follows the first in time, but what does this amount to? Lots of things succeed lots of other things and most of the time you aren't inclined to say that one is for the sake of the other. Suppose the clock strikes noon and the moment it stops I sneeze. You would not infer that the clock stopped for the sake of my sneeze. So why here—why think that going ashore is for the sake of laying eggs? For all we know, God might have chosen something else as the purpose of the turtles' going ashore. Maybe He has established from the foundation of time that turtles go ashore for the sake of compacting the sand as they walk. This theological picture of the world is one in which its real purposes are undisclosed, known to God alone and to whomever He reveals the secrets. The commonsense way of reading purposes in common occurrences—the tendency to think that the dolphin surfaces in order to breathe, that the birds gather twigs in order to build a nest—yields no true insight because, even if God's purposes happened to be what common sense tells us they are, we would have no way of knowing (short of a special divine disclosure) that in these cases his purposes happened to accord with common sense.

I once visited what I had every reason to think was a Catholic bookstore. I walked in and there everything was, the prayer books, Bibles, holy cards, books and pamphlets on abortion, the family, and the saints; rosaries, baptismal gowns, inspirational plaques—the whole show. But something was wrong. The store was untidy. It was dusty and dimly lit. Merchandise was old and worn. The proprietor seemed completely uninterested in my presence, and I was the only customer in the store. In fact, it felt as if I were intruding; something else was going on, it seemed. And so it was. I later learned that the shop had been raided by the police on suspicion of being a front for illegal drug-dealing. Maybe the proprietor read somewhere that religion is the opiate of the masses and got inspired.

If the purposes God assigns to actions in nature are not somehow linked with the natural pattern of things, then the whole natural world is just a front. What's really going on is very different from what the ordinary human observer cannot help but think is going on.

PURPOSES AND FINAL CAUSES

Bl. John agrees with very little of all this, I'm happy to say. I raise the nightmare possibility of God's alien purposes for the natural world merely in order to see by contrast what Scotus in fact thinks. But his own view does jive with the scary view I've been describing in one crucial respect. Yes, he does think that in general the true purposes of things are just whatever a thing's nature naturally suits it for. And yes, he therefore thinks in general that the true purposes of things are just what we humans can discover are the purposes of things. Still, it cannot be denied that God, according to Scotus, retains the prerogative to intend for things purposes other than what their natures best suit them for. The Scotistic rule of thumb here is that when God does assign alien purposes, it tends to work out for the better. In the remainder of this chapter I want to show how Scotus navigates this tension between, on the one hand, what we assume nature's purposes to be on the basis of observation and, on the other hand, God's freedom to set whatever purposes He likes.

Now, Scotus's concept of what I have so far been calling "purpose" is derived from Aristotle, and while Scotus transformed Aristotle's understanding of purpose, he freely used Aristotle's philosophical vocabulary, and never wholly discarded Aristotle's meaning. So a brief review of the relevant Aristotelian terminology is worth our while. Aristotle famously said that anything that comes into existence is caused and that any caused material thing has four kinds of causes. What Aristotle meant by "cause" is closer to what we mean by "explanation." The stuff out of which something is made is a cause—the material cause. The form of the thing is a cause—the formal cause. For example, consider scissors. Scissors need to be made of hard, durable material which can be sharpened; otherwise they wouldn't be able to perform typically scissory activity. Steel is the right sort of material, so we can call it the material cause or explanation of what makes this particular pair truly a pair of scissors. But a random chunk of steel is obviously not a pair of scissors. Something more than the steel is required for there to be scissors. The something more is, of course, the peculiar shape or form of scissors. Without this form, there would be no scissors, so we call the form a cause, a formal cause. The final two types of causes we have encountered already, in the chapter on God's existence: the agent which produced the thing is a cause—the efficient cause (from which we get our word *effect*); and the end or purpose of the thing is a cause—the final cause. So, for example, consider the nineteen-foot-tall statue of Abraham Lincoln in the Lincoln Memorial. Its material cause is marble, its formal cause is a likeness of Lincoln, its efficient cause is Daniel Chester French, and its final cause is to represent and honor the sixteenth President of the United States. Most relevant to our study here is, of course, the final cause. Purposes, Aristotle thinks, are a kind of *cause* of things whose purposes they are.

As stated, however, it seems very strange to call the purpose of a thing its cause, or one of its causes. Scissors are for cutting, and cutting only happens once you have the scissors. But causes, we suppose, are prior to their effects. Since the scissors are prior to the cutting, and not the other way around, it looks like cutting can't be a cause of the scissors. Nor do we want to say that something else's cutting (some other scissors, let's say) is a cause of these scissors, because something else's cutting is simply not relevant to these scissors. So if there is cutting prior to the scissors, it's not relevant to the causal process that produces the scissors; and if there is cutting after the scissors, it arrives on the scene too late to have been involved in the causal process that produced the scissors.

But Aristotle, despite what Vizzini says in *The Princess Bride*, is not a moron. In what non-moronic way, then, could he have thought of cutting as a cause of the scissors? This way: cutting, the scissors' purpose, is the reason scissors are made. Whatever their efficient cause, be they mass-produced in a factory or forged by hand in a metalworker's shop, if the factory or the metalworker are producing scissors they are producing them for cutting. Yes, there might be other reasons for producing them: to make money, for the love of the craft, and so on; but for the production to be a production of scissors rather than something else, cutting must be among the reasons they are made. So the scissors' purpose is a cause of the scissors when it is the reason their efficient cause produces them. Now this makes some sense. Sometimes we even talk of reasons or purposes as behaving like efficient causes. We might say that an artist is *moved* by some idea or picture in her mind to produce her artwork. We might say that C. S. Lewis, the efficient cause of the *Chronicles of Narnia*, was *moved* by a spontaneous mental image of a parcel-carrying faun with an umbrella under a lamppost to write his beloved stories.

But you might have noticed that, in order to make any sense of how a thing's purpose can be thought of as one of its causes, we had to resort to examples involving things made by humans. We know what it's like to make things, and we know what it's like to makes things for reasons. We're intelligent critters, at least some of the time, and therefore possess this mysterious power to see in our mind's eye a thing that doesn't yet exist, and then use this mental vision as a model and inspiration for producing, outside the mind, the thing we foresaw. As far as we know, however, we humans are the only animals endowed with this power. So—as Scotus's argument for a First Final Cause shows us—it is no simple matter to make intelligible the idea that a purpose can be a cause of a thing, when the efficient cause of a thing lacks this mental power. The coupling of a he-bear and a she-bear does indeed have a purpose—the wee bear—but it is hard to see how the wee bear can be a cause of the coupling, given that, one, it happens as a result of the coupling, and two, it cannot be held in mind by the couple as a reason to couple, because they have no minds to hold it in.

Having no interest in divorcing the bears, Scotus instead divorced two concepts which had long been held to be inseparable. On the one hand there is a thing's purpose;

on the other hand there is that thing's final cause, which is whatever it is that brings it about for the sake of that purpose. And he held that the natural purpose of a thing might fail to be the final cause of a thing—and this was his most radical departure from Aristotle's framework of the four causes. As Scotus saw it, in order for a purpose to be a cause, it must be loved, and a necessary condition for a thing's being loved is its being held in mind. So a purpose is a cause when some agent has that purpose in mind and brings something about for that purpose. What this means for the bears, on the assumption that they do not have minds for purposes to be in, is that even if the purpose of their coupling is the wee bear, the final cause of their coupling must be something external to the bears, something like this: God loved the wee bear so much that he brought about the coupling of the he-bear and she-bear, in part, for the purpose of making the wee bear. Wee bear remains the purpose of the coupling, but the final cause of the coupling is in God—more specifically, God is the final cause of the wee bear insofar as He brings about the coupling out of love for the wee bear which is brought about by the coupling.

Here is a different illustration of the same point about the distinction between purposes and final causes, a familiar illustration adapted from an earlier chapter. A spider spins in order to make a web, and the web is for catching bugs. And catching bugs is for eating. But the spider cannot have the thought, "I will spin a web in order to catch bugs." So there is no mental entity in the spider for the love of which the spider spins, and therefore, by Scotus's lights, there is nothing in the spider that is the final cause of the spider's web. This is not to say, however, that the spider's web has no final cause. Since we cannot locate the final cause "inside" the efficient cause (the spider), we must locate it elsewhere, in some mind. God, says Scotus, loves the spider's web and therefore produces the spider, in part, so that she will spin Him this web He foresaw; but God also loves the spider and therefore produces the spider so that she will spin her web so that she can catch bugs so that she can eat so that she can go on doing other spidery things. Out of love for these ends, God wills all the means to the ends. God, of course, could feed the spider all by himself, without any webs at all. But what He wills is not just any old food source for his spider but a web spun by the spider herself. So He produces the long chain of means necessary—necessary in the order of nature, anyway—for bringing about the nourishment of this very spider by this very web. So, yes, the spinning has a natural purpose: the web, and the web has a purpose, and so on; and the spinning also has a final cause, but its final cause is the divine idea of the web, beloved by God. Scotus would doubtless marvel with Jonathan Edwards who, meditating on the Mystery of the Flying Spider, exclaimed, "We hence see the exuberant goodness of the Creator, who hath not only provided for all the necessities, but also for the pleasure and recreation of all sorts of creatures, and even the insects and those that are most despicable."

FOUND OBJECTS

It is fashionable these days to reclaim and repurpose old stuff. Recently, I visited a warehouse in downtown Los Angeles in which young mustachioed men in flannel shirts were taking wood from demolished Midwestern barns and transforming it into flooring. In a magazine a couple years back I saw a bed which was little more than a mattress resting on a stack of shipping pallets. Thrift-shop teapots have become flower pots, empty gin bottles have become vases, trunks have become coffee tables, old doors have become headboards—the list is practically endless. In all these examples, something produced at some time for one purpose is now being used for some other purpose.

This trend gives us some insight into an important aspect of Scotus's understanding of the purposes of things. You can take your old teapot and make it a flower pot whenever you like and for whatever reason. You cannot take a single drop of ink and make it a flower pot, no matter your reason or however badly you want to. You can do the former because teapots, though their nature best suits them for pouring tea, are also naturally suited for holding soil and plants. But you can't make a drop of ink into a flowerpot. This is not because drops of ink happen to be better suited for staining porous media like paper than for holding soil and plants. It is because they aren't suited at all for holding soil and plants. Another reason you can repurpose your teapot is that you have authority over it: you own it, and it's the sort of thing you can do just about whatever you want with.

Every creature is to God as artifacts like teapots are to us. He has invented them; He has made them; they are his. None is owed anything from Him; none is more important than He. It is written (paraphrased), "Woe unto him who strives with his Maker, a teapot with the potter. Does the clay say to him who fashions it, What are you making?" (Isaiah 45:9). The only limits to what God can do to and with things are the limits imposed by the natures of things. Could God in his omnipotence engineer some way of making an ink drop a flowerpot? Maybe, but it's far-fetched: freeze the ink drop into the shape of a pot; insert very very small bits of soil and a very very tiny plant, which can live in freezing temperatures. Could God engineer some way of making a single O_2 molecule a flowerpot? Almost certainly not, since for something to be a flowerpot a plant must fit inside it, and no plant could fit inside a single O_2 molecule. This sort of restriction aside, God can bestow on a thing or an action any purpose He desires and, for that matter, can bestow on a thing several purposes at once. In short, while it is impossible for God to set a purpose for a thing that is clean contrary to the purposes given by a thing's nature, it is possible for God to set a purpose for a thing that is different from or beyond what its nature best suits it for.

It's not hard to imagine examples of divine repurposing. Here's one: the cross. Says the cross in the once-famous Anglo-Saxon poem "The Dream of the Rood":

> Now mayest thou know, beloved man, what deed of evil I have suffered, what grievous woes. Now bliss is come, so that men revere me far and wide throughout the earth, and all the great Creation prayeth to this beacon. On me the Son of God suffered a little time; wherefore in glory now I tower up beneath the sky; and I may bring healing unto every one of those that have regard for me. Of old was I the bitterest of tortures, loathsome to men, ere that I opened unto mortal men the true way of life. Lo! The Prince of glory, the Warden of the heavenly realm, hath shewed me honour over all the forest trees.

On a similar theme there is the sad but beautiful song by Elliott Park, which tells the story of a young oak tree which "like all other saplings . . . had dreams of growing strong and tall." But then a dying soldier hangs his heavy rifle on one of the sapling's limbs as he rests against its trunk and sings "Amazing Grace," before dying. The rifle remained, and its weight warped the natural growth of the young oak, so that as it grew and matured its trunk was arched. The oak was sad that it wasn't straight and tall. But "then one day two men came with a cross-cut saw / They spoke of how my arch would hold a weight so strong." These men fell the tree and subject it to "the hewer's careful blade." After long endurance the oak is happy with how its life turned out, despite its natural expectations:

> Now I'm the wooden arch that holds a mighty bell
> Three stocks before me cracked but I shall never fail
> Up in a tall cathedral high above my dreams
> Of long ago.

And on Sunday mornings when I hear that sweet refrain
I see the soldier's face like it was yesterday
Calling angels down from heaven with that hymn he softly sang
Of God's good grace.

Another example is Hosea's marriage to Gomer. Hosea and Gomer were husband and wife and so the purpose of their relationship, according to the *Book of Common Prayer*, was, first, for the procreation of children; second, for a remedy against sin; and third, for the mutual society, help, and comfort that the one ought to have of the other. We trust that God willed these for their marriage, and hence these things, as loved by God, were final causes of their marriage. But we know there was more going on here: "And the Lord said to Hosea, Go, take unto thee a wife of whoredoms and children of whoredom: for the land hath committed great whoredom, departing from the Lord" (Hosea 1:2). God gives Hosea the reason for taking Gomer as his wife: "for the land hath committed great whoredom" (Hosea 1:2). Hosea's marriage is supposed to be a symbol of God's faithfulness and Israel's faithlessness. Probably God intends all the natural purposes of marriage along with this symbolic purpose; otherwise it couldn't be the symbol it was ordained to be. It remains, however, that God has ordered their marriage to a purpose we could not guess, that is alien to whatever we could reasonably surmise, by our natural reason, about the marriage itself.

We could pile on examples, but I trust the point has been made. Outside of divine revelation we can't be sure of other real-life examples, but divine revelation teaches us not to be surprised if what God is up to in nature is something other than the naturally discernible purposes of things. Still, most of us would want to avoid a picture of the world in which everything seems to mean one thing and really means something rather different, like the "Catholic bookstore" I visited a few years ago. Scotus does too and thinks he has good reason to think that the created world is not just one big "Catholic bookstore." It is, he says, reasonable that God's purposes for a thing match those activities for which its nature best suits it. And God is reasonable. In general, it doesn't make sense to use an egg as a paperweight, because eggs are better suited for eating or for becoming chickens. Considering merely natural purposes, it doesn't make sense, as in Wonderland, to use flamingos as croquet mallets and hedgehogs as croquet balls. We could cook up some circumstance in which this does make sense, but it takes a flight of fancy to think how doing so is a good idea. We wouldn't want to say, however, that God wouldn't do such a thing as to will the flamingo into existence for the sake of being a croquet mallet. We know that He could do such a thing, and under an appropriately elaborate set of circumstances we can imagine why He might do such a thing. There is a story waiting to be written about the time when a boy's croquet mallet was switched mysteriously with a planking flamingo, who could talk. As the boy has his back turned to his opponents the flamingo in his hands whispers words of instruction which help the boy win the match and a kiss from the girl he admires. The boy and girl grow and up and get married and live happily ever after—and all because he played croquet with a flamingo. For God to ordain that this flamingo's purpose is to be used as a croquet mallet is, in the story, not just possible but reasonable, on the supposition that God wills for the boy and girl to fall in love and live happily ever after.

To return to the beginning, given facts about the natures of things like birds, bears, snakes, squirrels, and bees, it is reasonable for us to think that their purposes are just those activities for which their natures best suit them. And given that God is reasonable, it's reasonable for us to suppose that, under normal conditions, those activities really are their final causes, where we understand a final cause to be that out of love for which God brings something about. But Scotus teaches us that, given God's authority over all He has made, given his knowledge of all things, all activities of all things, and all the connections between things, God might be up to something besides the obvious.

8

TWO AFFECTIONS OF THE WILL

> Merry crawled on all fours like a dazed beast, and such a horror was on him that he was blind and sick. "King's man! King's man!" his heart cried within him.... But his will made no answer, and his body shook.... Then pity filled his heart and great wonder, and suddenly the slow-kindled courage of his race awoke. He clenched his hand. She should not die, so fair, so desperate! At least she should not die alone, unaided.... Suddenly [the Black Rider] stumbled forward with a cry of bitter pain, and his stroke went wide, driving into the ground. Merry's sword had stabbed him.
>
> —J. R. R. Tolkien, *The Lord of the Rings*

> The affection for justice is nobler than the affection for the advantageous, understanding by "justice" not only acquired or infused justice, but also innate justice, which is the will's congenital liberty by reason of which it is able to will some good not oriented to itself. According to the affection for what is advantageous, however, nothing can be willed save with reference to self.
>
> —Bl. John Duns Scotus, *Ordinatio*

> A free choice is nothing other than a choice which is able to keep uprightness-of-will for the sake of this uprightness itself.... To keep uprightness-of-will for the sake of uprightness itself is, for everyone keeping it, to will what God wills him to will.
>
> —St. Anselm of Canterbury, *On Freedom of Choice*

FREEDOM FROM WANTS

Bl. John's understanding of human freedom suggests that something besides the obvious is indeed going on. Many would be willing to admit that freedom is a necessary condition for morality. Fewer would be prepared to grant that morality is a necessary condition for freedom. But the latter is very nearly what Scotus himself does grant, and his doctrine of human freedom is the extension, into human affairs, of that unsettling possibility that God means more for a creature than its merely natural condition could ever suggest.

It is easy to neglect the logical connection between freedom and morality. But it is impossible to have a coherent understanding of what it even means for us to be free if you leave out what it means to be moral. Some people make the mistake of thinking that freedom means being able to do what you want to do. This is a very strange mistake, to think that freedom and wanting are connected like this. Demonstrably, being able to do what you want to do just cannot work as a definition of freedom. For suppose you were not free to form the wants that you have. Suppose, to be more specific, that you are completely caused by external forces to want a glass of water right this minute. And suppose that you indeed have the ability to do what you want to do. Well, then, you'd try to get the water. But it would make no sense to say that your *freedom* consists in your ability to do what you want—in this case, to get water—because the want itself is totally determined for you. Well, you might reply, fine then: let's say instead that freedom is the ability to do what you *freely* want to do. But this isn't a good definition, either, because the very concept we're trying to define shows up in this new definition. We would then be forced to say something about what it means to want something freely, and we'd be back right where we started.

The mystery of our freedom is somewhat less mystifying when we observe it in those circumstances in which we act *against* what we want: when you really want that greasy cheeseburger, for example, but you refrain, because you also want something else. There are these two wants, let us say: eating the cheeseburger, and giving the cheeseburger to your neighbor who has none, and you exercise your freedom when you *decide between* these wants. Let's suppose in our cheeseburger circumstance that sharing is pretty clearly the correct thing to do: you have just eaten a cheeseburger yourself and are in fact full, and your neighbor has eaten nothing all day, has no food of his own, and is seated right across the table from you; pretty clearly—I hope—the right thing to do is to share your cheeseburger with him. Of course, there is no physical necessity which follows upon this moral necessity and forces you to share. You are in fact free to share or not to share, to eat or not to eat. It is not really up to you, here and now, in the moment of desire, whether the cheeseburger will go on appealing to you so strongly. Nor is it up to you whether it's right or wrong to share your cheeseburger—the details of your circumstance which make it right for you to share have nothing to do with your wants. What options there are in addition to eating and sharing are there for you to recognize, not create. So we can say that the options available to you to choose between, however many there are, are not up to you. Instead, it's up to you to choose between them. It is not enough, then, to say that freedom is the ability to do what we want. Additionally, at least, freedom is the power to choose between competing wants.

WILLING ANOTHER'S WILL

But not even this power to choose between competing wants sufficiently captures what our distinctive human freedom consists in. I could offer a bowl of dry food, a bowl of wet food, or a rawhide chew toy to my dog. Imagine him sniffing each in turn, and after a few seconds digging into the wet food. The dog cannot ask itself, "Is this good?" or "Is this what I ought to be doing?" But we can. Of course we don't always ask it, and think of the stomachaches and headaches and heartbreaks that so often follow upon not asking. But we can ask, and we can answer the question. And sometimes the answer is not at all to our liking. And then we discover what it really means to be free: not enslaved to our passions but free to indulge or deny them, to discern whether here and now is the time to feed or play like one more of God's beasts or to lay animal indulgence aside for some other purpose. Perhaps it was not wrong for Prince Hal as Prince Hal to be frivolous, but there came a time when it would have been wrong to go on being Prince Hal, and that is the time when he really became King Henry. The burden of freedom is like the burden of royalty: it is only really felt when we enter that liminal state in which we recognize, deep down, that to go on living merely as I feel like living is not a good enough way to live. There are good things to be done that do not appear to be good for me, and, what is more, some of these good things to be done appear, in all fairness, to be more important than whatever I might do merely for my own good.

To understand Duns Scotus on the freedom of the will we must understand this human power of recognizing the good that is not just good for me and, perhaps not knowing whether it is at all good for me, choosing it anyway. There is no profounder merely human instance of this distinctively Scotist understanding of true freedom than Mary's *yes*: *fiat mihi secundum verbum tuum*; "let it be unto me according to thy word." That teenage girl espoused to Joseph heard a voice in her bedroom uttering strange words which she understood but did not fully comprehend. Her request for an account of how this great thing should be was met by the angel with no philosophical or scientific description of the causal mechanism by which a virgin would give birth to Emmanuel. God will do it, was the only answer. Yet Mary met the angel's *it shall be* with her own *let it be*, and this was the truest act of human freedom until, a little over thirty years later, Jesus Christ knelt in the Garden of Gethsemane and asked the Father to let the cup of crucifixion pass from him—*nevertheless, not my will, but thine be done.* Mary's permission made possible the Incarnation of the Word, and Christ's permission made possible the Redemption of the World, and so their words are the testimony of human freedom as it was meant to be.

A dog that chooses the moist morsel over the kibble alters the course of history, at least a little bit. Things go on from that moment in some ways differently from how they would have gone had that not occurred. Our own free actions alter history, too, but in our exercise of freedom we get to ask ourselves not just, "What do I want to do?" but, "How ought history go on from this moment?" What are the good ways for things in general to be, and how do the options before me here and now promote or fail to promote the goodness of things in general? Scotus insists that by reflecting on the natures of things we really can discern what is good and bad for them, and so develop robust ideas about how things in general ought to be. And through Scripture and Tradition we learn something of what God wills for our willing. Thus, if we are attentive to goods besides our own good, and are appropriately moved by them, we can use our freedom for others' good, and not just our own.

We really can recognize that while our own happiness does matter, it is not the most important thing in the universe. I am not worth making the center of my life, in the strict sense that I am not *worthy* to be the top-of-the-line object of *anyone's* willing, even my own. Having the rather intimate relationship of identity to myself does not in the least make it permissible to value my own happiness higher than the happiness of any other person. Ezra Pound once imagined what it would be like to be a very selfish ant: "the ant's a centaur in his dragon world." Scotus's response to the selfishness that locks us in our own dragon worlds is the same as Pound's: "pull down thy vanity, I say pull down." It is not only immoral but ridiculous to pretend, by your inordinate self-willing, that you are that for the sake of which all things ought to be willed.

There is a merciful side to this otherwise severe doctrine that we ought to love ourselves only as much as we are worthy of love. Since God is the Good Itself, there is no nobler exercise of freedom than to repeat in our willing what God wills us to will. It's not quite right to say that we should will whatever God wills, because it would be wrong of us to will everything God wills exactly as God wills it. But we should will what, and as, God wants us to will, to the extent we can have any knowledge about what He wills for our willing. And this is the spoonful of sugar in Scotus's bitter medicine: what God wills for us is loving union with himself, a union which consists of knowledge of God's essence fructified in the will's enjoyment of what is known. This union is the highest happiness a human being or angel is capable of. This is what God wills for our willing: that we love God above all things and for his own sake, and in so doing achieve supreme happiness. So while it would be wrong so intensely to will our own happiness, acting on our own authority, it is not wrong—in fact it is obligatory—so intensely to will our happiness as an act of obedience to the God who is the highest authority. Mary uses her will to will another's will, and as a result is blessed among woman. And, bad as it was at Gethsemane, we know that it was "for the joy set before him" that Christ willed to will the Father's will, knowing full well the suffering he was about to endure. So in our own little annunciations and passions, we can have some confidence that in our ending is our beginning: the terrible choice you know you must make but which you are sure will destroy you—it won't, by God's mercy. But to see why it won't, I think we need to dig down a bit deeper into the theoretical background of Scotus's understanding of the will.

A DEVILISH THOUGHT EXPERIMENT

In his own theorizing about this mysterious and daunting power of *willing* which God has bestowed on us, Duns Scotus was deeply influenced by a fanciful thought experiment conducted by the twelfth-century Benedictine monk and sometime Archbishop of Canterbury St. Anselm. Anselm applied his considerable dialectical powers to make some sense out of primordial sin. This is not the sin of Adam by which the human race fell into the slavery of sin, but the sin of Lucifer, by which he fell like lightning from heaven and became the serpent in Eden which tempted our first parents away from life in the earthly paradise. The intellectual problem of primordial angelic sin is considerable. Traditionally, Lucifer was taken to be the greatest, or one of the greatest, of the angels. Like all God's original creations, Lucifer was created good, and endowed with great power and great intelligence. We might speculate that no created person has ever had a nature so apt for persevering in the love of God, so apt for resisting any possible temptation. Yet he fell. What could explain this fall?

The traditional answer is *pride*. The angel, great as he was, was not content with his station. He wanted even more glory, more knowledge, more power, more admiration from his fellows. Consider: if God is infinitely good, then no matter how great He makes a creature, the gap between the greatness of that creature and God's greatness is still an infinite gap. And this means, plausibly, that God *could have* made any creature, even Lucifer, much greater than He in fact made him. So why didn't God make this—and every other creature, for that matter—much greater than He in fact did? Looked at from this angle, it might seem rather stingy of God to have made things the way He did, not nearly as great as He could have made them.

And this stinginess, if it is stinginess, could prompt a thoughtful creature to become jealous of God's infinite, unapproachable glory. And this jealousy could in turn breed envy, turning his longing for something he does not have into misery about the fact that God does have it, darkening the joy even of the greatest angel of the light. Of course, if he believes he does not deserve any of the good things he has, it is unlikely in the extreme he would go on to think he deserves any of the greater things he does not have. But if in his pride he does believe that he is owed the greater goods, and reflects that God could have given them but chose not to, then in his pride he will judge God stingy, and become jealous, envious, and finally resentful of his God. This hatred of God makes him unfit for heaven, and so he leaves, or is forced to leave (in the end there is not much difference). Wherever the lightning goes when it falls from the sky, we know this at least by experience: its great energy is no longer visible, and illuminates nothing.

Still, there is something psychologically unsatisfying in this story of Lucifer's fall. Left unexplained here is how someone so good could so much as start making the flawed acts of willing which put him on the road to hell. How does the descent get going? This is the problem Anselm set himself. For his solution he begins by considering what Lucifer's will must have been like, in its original goodness, if, despite the goodness, it was capable of sinning. Suppose, as many ancient philosophers supposed, that we only ever will what we believe will promote our own happiness and well-being. After all, Aristotle said long ago that happiness is the single ultimate end of every human action. Perhaps it is the same with angels. If so, then we can understand why Lucifer would have willed to be greater than he was made to be: it was in his nature to will what is good for him, so it is plausible that upon recognizing he could be made even better, he would desire this extra portion of goodness for himself. But Anselm recognized the catch: if happiness-desiring is what Lucifer's will was made to do, then he could not be *faulted* for desiring a greater station. To fault him would be as senseless as faulting a plant for growing only in the direction of the light. A plant which gives itself an imbalanced shape by its striving toward the sun is not to be blamed for doing so, since it is not the sort of thing that could do otherwise.

So we must characterize this angelic will in some way which makes it sensitive to *right and wrong*, able to judge what ought to be done, whether or not it promotes his own happiness. Imagine a creature so intelligent that it always correctly judged the right thing to be done, in every circumstance in which it found itself. And imagine this same creature endowed with a will that could will only whatever the creature judged to be the right thing to do. Then indeed the creature would without fail will the right thing, and never fall. It is also possible to imagine a creature with a will just as steadfastly fixed on what is right, but coupled to an intellect which did not reliably judge correctly about matters of right and wrong. The will, upright as it is, depends on the judgments of reason for its movement toward this or that object. If that reasoning capacity errs, however, and presents to the upright will an option which is in fact wrong but as though it were right, then the upright will would go for it all the same. The will literally does not know any better; it is not the power for knowing but the power for pursuing whatever the intelligence declares to be the thing to be done.

If we imagine Lucifer with just such a will, but unfortunately coupled to a defective intelligence, we would indeed get an explanation of how such a being could make mistakes: the problem is in the intellect, not the will. But this won't actually do as a solution to the problem of Lucifer's original sin, for at least two reasons. First, while it is easy to see that a person who did the wrong thing, believing it to be the right thing, is in fact mistaken, it is impossible to imagine that such a person could actually be blamed for that mistake. He is not responsible for the intellectual error which led to the mistake; his will was up to the task of righteousness, but he was given low-grade intellectual equipment, and so failed. It is unfortunate, but he is not really blameworthy. Second, the tradition has held that Lucifer's intelligence was more than adequate for judging the right thing to be done. Indeed, we should think of him as one of the smartest created persons whom God has ever made. So if we're going to get a satisfying solution to the problem of Lucifer's sin, we must look elsewhere.

Anselm's ingenious solution involves attributing to Lucifer's will—and by extension to all created wills—two basic inclinations. On the one hand, we do indeed desire what is good for us; Anselm calls this the *affection for what is advantageous* (*affectio commodi*). But on the other hand, we also desire what is right, whether or not we recognize that it is good for us; and Anselm calls this the *affection for what is just* (*affectio iustitiae*). To have a will is to be inclined toward both of these, and not just one or the other. The sense of freedom that matters for Anselm is not just that we are the source of our own actions but that we are genuinely praiseworthy for the good we choose to do and blameworthy for the bad we choose to do. And I can only be so if we can really recognize the good in both acting in my own self-interest and acting for the sake of things other than myself. If I share my cheeseburger with you I might remain a little hungry after our meal, and I'll get less overall pleasure from the meal. But you'll be less hungry than you are now, and you'll get to share in the pleasure I would have had all by myself. As an Anselmian agent, I am, by the very nature of my will, drawn both to the good things I can get by keeping the burger for myself and to the good things you will get if I share it with you. Even in cases where there is no apparent good for me—paradigmatically, cases in which acting for another's sake means risking injury or death—there is still that within me which is drawn to the goodness of the risky option. People who act for the sake of others in these paradigmatically heroic cases are not, on Anselm's view, suppressing their own will and yet miraculously choosing to do the heroic thing. Instead, these heroes are *choosing between* native drives of their own God-given will: in these cases, choosing the option which is for someone else's good.

As with all created wills, so with Lucifer's: he had these twin native drives in his own will. He really did have an inclination for what was in his own self-interest. And he also really had an inclination to those good things which were not in any clear sense connected to his own self-interest. He also had extraordinary intelligence. Thus, he would have known that while it was indeed possible for God to have made Lucifer even greater than he was, he also would have known that God is the sovereign ruler of all creation, and therefore that God's will is to be followed even when we cannot see how it is good for me to do so. His originally good will would have responded, by nature, to all this knowledge by having inclinations both to an ever-more exalted status in heaven and to God's sovereign choice to make Lucifer as He did and no higher. That inclination to a higher status was not in itself wrong: that was just the *affectio commodi* doing its natural thing; also, the inclination to respect God's will was not in itself saintly: it was just the *affectio iustitiae* doing its natural thing. Lucifer's freedom consisted in that power he had to prefer the object of one of these inclinations over the other, and to act or be prepared to act so as to secure it. And we all know how he used that power: he preferred a more exalted status for himself and he would have done what he could to secure it. In this particular case, there was nothing he could have done: he wanted something only God could give him, and God didn't want to give him that thing. So willing his own exaltation was bound to lead to frustration. And now our earlier tale about God's apparent stinginess leading to jealousy, envy, resentment, and hatred makes more sense.

But after all, this story only seems to make sense of how Lucifer had the sort of knowledge and the sort of freedom he would have needed in order to go wrong. It doesn't seem to make much sense if we remember that Lucifer was supposed to be good. If he was so good—in addition to being so knowledgeable—how did he come to use his freedom to will contrary to God's willing? There are a couple things to be said here, one of which really shows that Anselm had a flair for the dramatic. As Anselm tells the tale, Lucifer knew that what he wanted was contrary to what God wanted him to want and was therefore wrong, but Lucifer did not know—and could not have known—what God would do in response to Lucifer's rebellious willing. Maybe God would punish, and if He did God would be right to do so. But maybe God would show mercy, and if He did this He would also be right. Lucifer was very smart, but he couldn't predict what God would freely do in return. So imagine Lucifer soliloquizing along these lines:

"I am inclined to want a higher status than the status God has willed for me. Only God can give it to me. If I actively will this higher status God will know all about it. Since it is contrary to his will and since God's will is perfectly righteous, I will become worthy of punishment, a punishment so severe that I would lose my place in heaven forever. But since God is also merciful, He might not punish me. He might leave me just as I am. Heck, He might even grant me what I really want! Maybe God will see me as the Persistent Widow and, like the Judge in that future parable, relent and begin to will for me what I will for myself. I cannot predict how God will respond.

It is in fact a gamble. But, oh, damn it all! I want that higher status so badly! I shall risk it. I will risk it all!"

Notice that Lucifer's deliberation here, up until the resolution to do the thing he knows is against God's will, is not in itself sinful. There's an obvious *direction* to the deliberation: he wants the wrong thing and is thinking how he could rationally and morally justify pursuing it. But even this directionality is not really sinful—or wouldn't be in Lucifer, who, we're supposing, hasn't yet committed that primordial sin for which he is so famous. But remember, the point of discussing Anselm's devilish thought experiment in detail is not to gossip about the devil but to reveal something to ourselves about own freedom. Like Lucifer and all the angels, we are created with wills which incline us in these two directions, towards what is just and towards what is advantageous. Not all the time, but sometimes, the objects of these inclinations are incompatible: the just thing here and now, in this particular case, is not advantageous. Freedom is that power we have to move decisively in one direction or the other.

What this power of freedom emphatically is not is a power to choose between servitude or self-rule. Milton's Satan declares, "*Non serviam*," I will not serve. But even if we take his word for it that it is better to rule in hell than serve in heaven, he still serves, even as the infernal tyrant. Dante portrayed Satan's unwilling submission to God's reign by placing him at the dead center of the cosmos, a winged beast whose flapping wings freeze the lake in which he, first traitor, forever munches on the worst of the worst of human traitors. He is God's bottom-rung executioner, with no hope of promotion. There's no getting out of serving, because the restriction built into the very nature of created being is that everything but God is the servant at least of God. No man can serve two masters, the scripture sayeth, and notice it doesn't offer what we modern people, and Satan, might think of as the logical alternative to serving one or more masters, namely, serving none at all. Scripture doesn't give us this out, because Scripture is always true to the deepest nature of creaturely reality, and that reality is subordination. So to understand freedom we've got to understand it as the power to choose what sorts of masters we will have, besides God whose mastery we can't actually escape. As Anselm puts it elsewhere, we can use our freedom to make ourselves slavish, like a man who freely walks into a prison cell. Or we can use our freedom to repeat in our wills God's will for our willing. In doing so we are the slaves of no angel or other man, not even a slave to ourselves. The fact is that I am not a worthy master, even of myself. The freedom for which God has made us free is to be the loyal subjects of Christ the King, lords and ladies of God's realm, noble but not sovereign.

VOLUNTARISM AND HAPPINESS

It is hard to overstate the importance of St. Anselm's two-affections theory of the will for Bl. John's own thinking. It is in fact the theoretical foundation of one aspect of Scotus's so-called *voluntarism* about the human will. I am not concerned with a precise definition of this technical term, but in this particular context, Scotus is a *voluntarist* about human willing in the sense that he thinks there is no single object which the human will necessarily strives for—not its own happiness, and not God. Scotus is as emphatic as any follower of Aristotle that a human being is inclined by nature to will its own happiness. And he is as emphatic as any Thomist that human happiness can only be found in God. Nevertheless, the will remains free to choose not just the means to its ultimate end, but even the ultimate end itself. But—and this is crucial for rectifying various misunderstandings of Scotus's so-called voluntarism—it is not in our power to make just anything at all our ultimate end. The choice of ultimate ends is between just two: self and God. All other choices are means. On Scotus's view it really is possible to will what God wants us to will because God wants us to will it, and not because we think that in doing so we will be happy. A person who achieves this sort of willing cannot in any meaningful sense be said to have her own happiness as the ultimate end of her willing. She wants what God wants her to want. Whether or not her own happiness is included—even necessarily included—in what God wants her to want is beside the point. In a paradox barely to be imagined by those of us who are very far indeed from seeking first the kingdom of God and his righteousness, this saint wills even her happiness for God's sake, and not for her own sake.

The two-affections theory explains this capacity to will something in this non-self-interested way. It says that while we are always by nature inclined to self-interest, we are also inclined to what is simply just, independent of how it affects our own well-being. By exercising our freedom to act in the direction of this affection for justice, we disregard our happiness, even if only temporarily. But that drive within us which looks out for our own interests is perfectly natural and God-given. It is not a disease of the will contracted by original sin, or anything like that.

The natural goodness of the *affectio commodi* is a clue to what God wants for our willing. There is hardly anything less attractive than an extremely self-denying and joyless person. If there is no joy in the labor, it can't really be called a labor of love. This is not to say that the hard work of loving God and neighbor is at every moment a sunset walk on the beach. Blood, sweat, tears, etc. No one knew better than Francis of Assisi how intense asceticism and intense joy could flourish in the same soil. The *Little Flowers of St. Francis* tells how Francis taught Brother Leo the source of true joy. It is not in being a good moral exemplar to the faithful, or in performing miracles, or in deep theological learning, or in converting the infidels. Nope. The source of true joy is to bear the sufferings of Christ for the love of Christ, enduring all suffering on earth as a way of participating in the suffering of Christ. His point, as I understand it, is that the love of Christ itself gives rise to joy, and that joy is unshakable, whatever one endures for Christ's sake.

Why should there be this connection between loving Christ and experiencing joy? The answer, I think, is that God wants us to have joy. Jesus tells us as much. He tells us that if we keep his commands we will remain in his love. And then he explains why he told us this: "These things I have spoken to you, that my joy may be in you, and that your joy may be full" (John 15:11). To repeat an earlier point which bears repetition, perfect obedience to God is to repeat in our wills God's will for our willing. So if what God wills for us is to be joyful, then we are acting contrary to our obedience not to will our own joy. In the hard and fast scale of value, we sit roughly in the middle, and the love we owe ourselves in pure justice is about middle-of-the-road love. God is infinitely above the highest creature on the scale, and therefore is owed by justice not just the greatest portion of our love, but that all our loves be ordered to the love of God, willing everything for God's sake. Yet what God can will for creatures is not bound by this hard and fast scale. He can, for example, will that middle-of-the-road creatures like us be fantastically blessed, beyond what we deserve. And this is the surprising thing about the joy Christ wishes for us. He doesn't owe us joy. It's pure liberality. There's no reason to it, in the sense of a reason which would make it rationally or morally incumbent on God to arrange for our well-being in this way. We surely cannot dare to desire our own happiness quite as much as God apparently desires our own happiness; but we could desire it a great deal and not come close to testing the limit.

All of this is in the background, I think, of Christ's startling extension of friendship to his servants the disciples (John 15:15). Christ is the first to know that this is not a friendship of true equals. But it is a real friendship because Christ really does will what is good for us, and we, as we grow in friendship with Christ, become more able to will what is good for him. Like true friends, we don't pridefully resist the good things our friends do for us. Accepting the asymmetry between us, in humility we welcome the extraordinary good that Christ accomplishes for us; and in humility Christ receives from us the meager offerings of love we are able to give him as so many kingly presents. In the give-and-take of friendship, in which even receiving good things from my friend takes on the character of acting generously toward my friend (since I am giving him what he wants by my willingness to receive good things from him), it seems to me that the two affections of the will, the *affectio commodi* and the *affectio iustitiae*, are simultaneously satisfied. That, anyway, is the goal of Christian life no less than a friendship, the goal St. Francis seems to have reached and the goal for which Duns Scotus provides a useful theoretical framework.

9

THE VIRTUOUS LIFE

Purity of heart is the will's freedom from all disordered delight.
—Bl. John Duns Scotus, *Ordinatio*

By faith a wayfarer is sufficiently perfected with respect to God as he is to be understood in this life.... With respect to God as worthy of love in himself, a wayfarer is sufficiently perfected by charity; and with respect to God as worthy of love for my own sake, as beneficial for me, hope perfects the wayfarer.
—Bl. John Duns Scotus, *Ordinatio*

The whole point about St. Francis of Assisi is that he certainly was ascetical and he certainly was not gloomy.... He devoured fasting as a man devours food. He plunged after poverty as men have dug madly for gold. And it is precisely the positive and passionate quality of this part of his personality that is a challenge to the modern mind in the whole problem of the pursuit of pleasure.... The stars which passed above that gaunt and wasted corpse stark upon the rocky floor had for once, in all their shining cycles round the world of labouring humanity, looked down upon a happy man.
—G. K. Chesterton, *St. Francis of Assisi*

SOUL FITNESS

We are clearly not the sort of people who would be very good at being friends with God; still less the sort of people who would enjoy it. So we need to undergo some soul training, training which is sometimes unpleasant, like physical training. St. Francis's familiar rigors, such as mixing ash in his bread and sleeping in the snow, are—I dearly hope—not compulsory, but they do provide us an exaggerated exemplar of the sort of discipline each of us should be willing to undertake. Bl. John was inspired by this sort of discipline, probably in his own life but certainly in the philosophical reflections on virtue he has left behind. We can learn a lot from that disciple of the complicated saint who endured physical agonies for the sake of spiritual health. In doing so, we can come to see that it was precisely out of love for the goodness of God's creation, including that bit of creation which was his own body, that Francis subjected himself to such torments. Franciscan self-discipline and self-denial are essentially positive, not negative: they aim at making us fully human. Beholding the ideal of a created order, joyful and flourishing, singing to God its Father, St. Francis and his followers wished to impose on themselves the sort of rigors that would help them be flourishing participants in that creaturely choir.

ANIMAL AND RATIONAL

A good place to start understanding how we ought to order our desires toward becoming fully human is what human nature itself is. In earlier chapters we have celebrated the mere fact we are human, and rightly so; and we have celebrated our individuality in our shared humanity, and rightly so. But now it is time to inquire what exactly this humanity is that makes us what, if not in all respects who, we are.

We human beings have a nature that is essentially embodied and animal, but also rational. We live our lives as a nexus of the material and spiritual worlds. As animals, we desire innately those things which are delightful and which meet our physical needs—objects of what Scotus and others call the *concupiscible appetite*—and we resist innately those things which are threatening—objects of the *irascible appetite.* These appetites are good, but all they do and are made to do is draw us toward or away from their proper objects. They cannot stop to ask themselves, so to speak, whether the things toward which they attract us really ought to be pursued, or whether the things from which they repel us really ought to be avoided. It is no fair to fault them for being dumb, for they were never made to speak for themselves but to be properly trained.

As *rational* animals, however, we do have the ability to stop and ask ourselves whether this pleasing object, just because it is pleasing, ought to be pursued; or that odious object, just because it is odious, ought to be avoided. We are not determined to follow the dictates of our physical appetites. We can step back, reflect, and deliberate about what, all things considered, is the good thing to do here and now. Sometimes deliberation will conclude that yes, indeed, we should pursue what is pleasing or avoid what is painful. But other times it will conclude just as rationally that, in some concrete circumstances, the thing to do is to avoid the pleasant and pursue the painful. Reason, not physical appetite, is the power by which we can direct our own course, informed by but not subjugated to physical appetite.

Our rationality involves two different but closely related powers: intellect and will. Think of intellect as our power of understanding and think of will—that power we considered in some detail in the previous chapter—as our power of pursuing or avoiding, loving or hating or being indifferent toward, whatever it is we understand. These powers are closely related in that the will is incapable of willing anything blindly; Scotus recognizes no such thing as a sheer act of unconditioned willing. Instead, the will can only operate on information presented to it by the intellect. This is why the will is the *rational appetite*. Despite this intimate connection, however, the will retains a profound freedom from the intellect in the sense that it is never bound to pursue or avoid, love or hate, anything the intellect presents to it. The intellect can sort through the various messy features of a complex deliberation and arrive at the good, or the good-enough, conclusion about what ought to be done, sometimes good enough that the will would be irrational and wrong not to choose to bring that conclusion into action. Nevertheless, despite the choice-worthiness of the intellect's conclusion, the will remains free to reject it—though, as we have seen in the last chapter, it is supremely free when it embraces it.

Intellect and will are intimately related in another way: the will can play a role in focusing the intellect's attention. Practically speaking, this sort of focused attention is necessary; in any concrete circumstances, there are infinitely many facts but only a few that are relevant to the deliberation about what to do. For example, if you have five tacos and your friend has none, one of the facts in this situation is that paper is made from trees. But this fact is not relevant to deciding whether to share your tacos with your friend. But suppose another of the facts in this situation is that your friend has no tacos because she ordered hers before you and she has already eaten them all. This is a relevant fact which may well lead you to conclude you needn't share your tacos with her. An undisciplined or vicious will is free to direct the intellect's attention to irrelevant facts, or relevant but selective facts; but a good will tries to direct the intellect's attention to all relevant facts. The will does not know anything apart from the intellect, but it can, so to speak, commission the intellect to search out relevant facts.

So far we have distinguished between a human being's animality and rationality, with animality characterized by the two physical appetites, the concupiscible and irascible; and rationality characterized by intellect and will, that is, the rational appetite. No single one of these powers is the person itself. It's not as though the will is the true subject of the "I" that acts. No, the "I" is the same thing as the human being. The human being understands with its intellect, chooses with its will, desires what is pleasing with its concupiscible appetite, and defies what is odious with its irascible appetite. All the powers of a human being are the sorts of things which can be disposed well or badly, and they are doing well precisely insofar as the person whose powers they are is thinking or acting well with respect to whatever sphere of thought or action that power is naturally ordered to.

TRAINING OUR POWERS

What is it, among things, which explains the difference between a good and a bad disposition of one of our powers? On Scotus's view, the answer is *habit*. A habit in its most general sense is the sort of thing which, added to something else, inclines it reliably toward some determinate types of objects. That I have a habit of drinking coffee, then, amounts to something in my body which inclines me reliably to drink coffee daily in the morning. The power of intellect and the three appetites (rational, concupiscible, and irascible) are themselves the kinds of things which can become subjects of habits. We call those habits *bad* which incline these powers reliably toward bad actions. Those habits are good which incline their powers to good actions. Because goodness itself is completion or perfection, good habits tend to make a person not just better than a person with bad habits but also *more fully human* than one with bad habits. Good habits perfect or complete our humanity.

We therefore become the sort of people who do what is right, in the right spirit, when we are perfected by those good habits which incline our powers and appetites toward what is good for us to think or do. We rightly call a bad habit a *vice* because it holds us back and weakens us; a good habit by contrast is a *virtue* because it strengthens and completes us. Quite literally, the vicious man is a weak man, and the virtuous man is a strong man—no matter how much each can bench-press.

THE TAXONOMY OF VIRTUE

In this most general sense of virtue, any habitual excellence is virtuous. Scotus says that even the mastery of individual subjects of knowledge, such as physics or mathematics, is virtuous in the sense that mastering these "disciplines" shapes the speculative intellect in a way that equips it reliably to contemplate truth (the truths to be found in each discipline) instead of falsehood. Knowing the truth is the natural object or goal of the speculative intellect, so those habits which equip it to reach that goal are, therefore, virtues—even if they don't have any distinctively moral value.

But the classical Christian understanding of the virtues focuses on seven: the four cardinal virtues: temperance, courage, justice, and prudence; and the three theological virtues: faith, hope, and love. The cardinal virtues are so named because of their importance among the virtues, and more importantly because of their fundamentality. Their fundamentality was recognized by the great pagan philosophers, Plato, Aristotle, and their successors; and many Church Fathers wove these pagan insights into a thoroughly Christian theology of character and spiritual formation. Within this broad tradition in which temperance, courage, justice, and prudence are fundamental, the many other virtues are but specifications of these cardinal virtues; for example, chastity is a species of temperance, that is, temperance in regards to sexual behavior, the virtue that bids the priest or religious be continent for life, the unmarried person be continent until marriage, and the married person love only his spouse and keep that love open to conceiving new life. As Scotus understands them, the proper subjects of the virtues are the highest powers of our soul—intellect and will—though these virtues of the will can lead to virtuous inclinations in our bodies too.

The theological virtues are so called both because they

directly concern our action toward God and because they are infused into the soul supernaturally by the grace of God, rather than acquired naturally through habitual good works. The *Catechism of the Catholic Church* describes these as the virtues which "adapt man's faculties for participation in the divine nature." The biblical source for this is St. Paul's famous conclusion to his great "Hymn to Love," in which he declares that three virtues endure: faith, hope, and love—with love the greatest of all (I Cor 13:13).

We can only make sense of the enduring emphasis on these seven virtues by understanding how they are habits that perfect human nature. Each virtue, whether cardinal or theological, must therefore be a habit that perfects a human power. Virtues, even when they have something to do with morality, are not merely about rule-following. Focusing on rules and rule-following can distract from the way in which the virtues are intimately related to what we human beings are. They are so many flowers typical of the human plant, which blossom in well-lived lives. Many of them do have something to do with doing the right thing, but more fundamentally than this, they have to do with becoming fully alive: the sort of people who can have joy in the midst of sadness and anxiety; eagerness to do good, and delight in doing good, and excellence in the performance of the good, even when circumstances are difficult or dangerous; and freedom from the tyranny of disorderly desires.

Thinking through Scotus's writings about the virtues, combined with his distinctively Anselmian theory of the will—discussed in the previous chapter—gives us an attractively tidy and powerfully explanatory way of visualizing the types of virtues which exhaustively perfect the powers of the human soul:

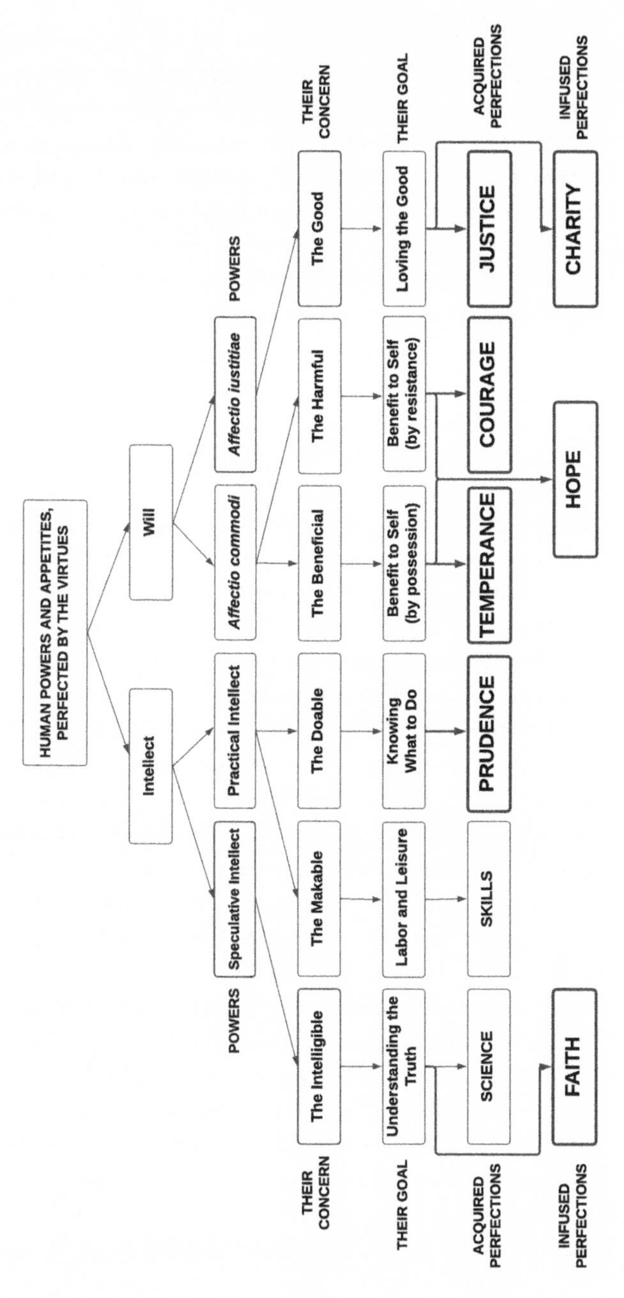
HUMAN POWERS AND APPETITES, PERFECTED BY THE VIRTUES
Intellect
Will
POWERS
Speculative Intellect
Practical Intellect
Affectio commodi
Affectio iustitiae
POWERS
THEIR CONCERN
The Intelligible
The Makable
The Doable
The Beneficial
The Harmful
The Good
THEIR CONCERN
THEIR GOAL
Understanding the Truth
Labor and Leisure
Knowing What to Do
Benefit to Self (by possession)
Benefit to Self (by resistance)
Loving the Good
THEIR GOAL
ACQUIRED PERFECTIONS
SCIENCE
SKILLS
PRUDENCE
TEMPERANCE
COURAGE
JUSTICE
ACQUIRED PERFECTIONS
INFUSED PERFECTIONS
FAITH
HOPE
CHARITY
INFUSED PERFECTIONS

Consider the two powers essential to human beings, intellect and will. We can distinguish between the speculative intellect and the practical intellect. The speculative intellect is concerned with that sort of knowledge which is good for its own sake and which is not necessarily related to any practical applications—though of course such knowledge may indeed have practical applications. It concerns the intelligible, or thinkable, and the object or goal of this power is truth, or perhaps the contemplation of the truth. The *acquired* habits which perfect this power, so that it reliably reaches its goal, are the variety of "scientific" disciplines familiar to Scotus from the liberal arts training he and his confreres received at Oxford: mathematics, physics, and metaphysics. But the *infused* habit which perfects this power specifically in relation to God is faith. Faith is that habit by which we firmly hold as true all that God has revealed of himself and his will for us, especially those truths which the speculative intellect could not have acquired on its own.

The practical intellect, by contrast, is concerned with practical applications, and these are of two basic sorts, each with its own object, what Scotus calls the "makable" and the "doable." First, there is the sort of intellectual activity that goes into our labor and hobbies. It concerns the makable, and the object or goal of this power is to order our physical environment in a way suitable for our flourishing. The habits which perfect this power are all the skills and crafts people acquire to work or play with greater ease and excellence: gardening, carpentry, musicianship, coding, and so on. Second, there is the sort of intellectual activity we do when we are thinking about what we should do. It concerns what is doable, and its goal is practical truth: truth about what is good and bad in action, what we must or must not do, what we may do, and so on—here and now in some concrete circumstance. Sometimes this is peculiarly moral deliberation, but not always. Should you work through lunch or take a break? Should you put on a movie for the kids or read them a story? When we work toward answers to questions like these, we're trying to arrive at a judgment about what we should do, and matters of moral right and wrong are not always at issue in these quotidian deliberations. The *acquired* habit which perfects this part of the practical intellect is the cardinal virtue of prudence. Prudence is that good habit by which we reliably attend to all relevant information in our deliberations, and by which we assign the right sort of weight to the various options that information opens to us.

On the side of the will there is also a twofold division, between the inclination for what is advantageous (*affectio commodi*) and the inclination for what is just (*affectio iustitiae*). This inclination for the advantageous concerns, you will be unsurprised to learn, that which is advantageous. It is that basic drive we all have to do or avoid whatever we need to do or avoid in order to be as well off as we can be. Therefore it is not just an inclination to pursue desirable things, but also an inclination to resist odious things. These two aspects of the affection for our own advantage are, then, the two appetites discussed earlier, the concupiscible and the irascible. The object or goal of the *affectio commodi* is, then, to possess beneficial things, so as to be made better off by them; and to avoid or destroy harmful things, so as not to be harmed by them. The *acquired* habits which perfect this inclination are, accordingly, temperance and courage. By temperance we habitually desire good things in a way that is really good for us. And by courage we habitually resist odious things in a way that is good for us. The *infused* habit which perfects this *affectio* is hope. Hope is that habit by which we are able to hold steadfast in our love for God, loving Him specifically for the good things we know He can and wants to do for us.

The inclination for what is just is our drive to be concerned about what is good and bad for other people (and things besides ourselves generally). On this broadly Anselmian view, we are not by nature egotistic. We can choose to be egotistic, by consistently preferring to will what we think is good for us, at the expense of willing what is good for others. But this egotism would be a *choice*, not an *instinct*. The point for Scotus is that this inclination toward others is a native power of the will, and so it too is the sort of inclination which is perfected by virtue. Its concern is the good of others; its object is to love other things as they deserve to be loved—and Scotus simply took it for granted that genuine love in this domain entails acting in certain ways, not just having certain loving feelings.

It might sound odd that an inclination like this, which by nature takes us outside ourselves and makes us mindful of others, would be the sort of power needing a perfecting habit. But it does need one. After all, it is possible to be deficiently or excessively concerned with another's good. Loving other things in their proper order, proportionate to their goodness, is difficult and requires training. Also, it is worth observing that one might be sufficiently concerned about others, and act with the intention to do good, but still fail to do what is in fact good for others. For example, if you are a charitable conservative, you might think that liberals benevolently but harmfully try to raise taxes; likewise, if you are an equally charitable liberal you might think that conservatives benevolently but harmfully try to lower taxes. The charitable liberal and conservative therefore agree that it is possible to be genuinely trying to act for another's good and yet fail to do so. What all this tells us is that the *affectio iustitiae* is yet another power which can be directed well or badly, and therefore is yet another power in need of a perfecting habit. The *acquired* habit of this inclination of the will is, you guessed it, justice. Charity is the infused habit of this same inclination toward what is just. Scotus calls charity the virtue whereby we love God not for the sake of the good things He gives us but for his own sake, because He is "all good and worthy of all our love," as we say in the Act of Contrition.

THE CONNECTION OF THE VIRTUES

For medieval theologians who wrote about the virtues, Aristotle's *Nicomachean Ethics* was an extremely important pagan source of inspiration. In addition to providing the conceptual framework in which thirteenth- and fourteenth-century authors thought about virtues, virtue acquisition, and virtuous action, Aristotle taught what is sometimes called the Unity Thesis, which is the thesis that the virtues are *unified* in such a way that it is impossible for anyone to have one virtue and lack any of the others—virtue is an all-or-nothing affair. Plato's Socrates had taught the Unity Thesis before Aristotle, but medieval authors were unfamiliar with all but a sliver of Plato's work.

A few examples can show the plausibility at first glance of the Unity Thesis. Consider that a very intemperate person might not have the willpower to act courageously if, for example, the courageous action would come at the expense of foregoing tasty treats. Intemperance is an obstacle to courageous action. Temperance, then, seems to be required for courage. Similarly, if prudence is the virtue which equips a person to perceive relevant circumstances here and now so as to deliberate well about what is to be done, then it sure seems that temperance, courage, and justice require prudence: how can a person act courageously, or temperately, or justly if he is not good at identifying the morally relevant circumstances of his realm of action?

Despite the initial plausibility of the Unity Thesis, there are also strong reasons for rejecting it. Most importantly, we know that we ourselves, and all those we know, have what we call strengths and weaknesses. You might have a real weakness for tacos—which indicates a lack of temperance—but nevertheless consistently do what justice requires, even when it comes to sharing tacos. Also, you might be pretty good at discerning what is to be done in certain circumstances—which indicates you possess prudence—but then frequently fail to carry out what you've concluded needs to be done, which suggests you lack the other cardinal virtues.

Bl. John rejected the Unity Thesis, but he does hold on to one important component of it. Importantly for Scotus, prudence is unlike the other three cardinal virtues in that the proper subject of prudence is, as we have already seen, the *intellect,* while the proper subject of the other three is the *will.* Scotus grants that having a rightly ordered will makes it easier to develop prudence. After all, if the will is habitually inclined to will rightly, it will direct the intellect's attention to the relevant aspects of circumstance. For example, you may have five tacos and a desire to eat them all, but you are also with a friend who has no food to eat, and this fact is relevant to your deliberation about what to do with those tacos. If your will is already inclined toward sharing your goods generously, you are more likely to focus your attention on your friend's lack and let this fact inform your deliberation about what to do with your tacos.

Nevertheless, Scotus holds that strictly speaking it is possible to have prudence without the other cardinal virtues, since prudence itself is simply the "habit that perfects the intellect in the domain of action," that is, in the domain of reasoning about what to do. But he believes that genuine freedom requires that the will be free to ignore the dictates of practical reasoning, whether those dictates are correct or incorrect. This means that from the mere fact that the intellect perfectly apprehends everything relevant to the domain of action and draws a conclusion about what is to be done, no particular act of willing follows, either for or against the practical intellect's conclusion.

So Scotus holds that you can be prudent without being temperate, courageous, or just. But he denies the converse. That is, he holds that you cannot be temperate, courageous, or just without prudence. As virtues of the will, these three virtues perfect the will's willing. But willing without reasoning is blind. For the will to will rightly in any given circumstances, it must be informed by the intellect what is the right thing to be done. For the will, then, habitually to will correct action—which is just what it means for the will to be virtuous—it must habitually receive from the intellect practical conclusions about what constitutes correct action—and the intellect can only offer this ongoing aid to the will if it is perfected by prudence.

The Unity Thesis concerns the relations between different virtues. But there is a second sense in which we might consider the unity of the virtues, namely, the unity, or disunity, of some particular virtue in itself. Scotus, for example, thinks of prudence as one generic kind under which fall many different virtues, all entitled to the name of prudence, but each having a discrete domain of action. One person might be practically wise in her relationships with other people, but practically unwise when it comes to financial matters, or vice versa. In this sense prudence is like art: a person may be an excellent musician but a poor painter; we might call the musician an artist on account of her musicianship, but in bestowing the title artist we don't mean to imply that she is proficient in all arts. The same thing with prudence: someone practically wise about relationships but not about money may rightly be called prudent, without implying that she is prudent in every respect. The various species of prudence are unified insofar as they are all species of the same genus, namely, a habit which perfects the intellect's ability to reason practically about what is to be done.

In fact, Scotus thinks that all the natural, acquired virtues are divided up like this. Strictly speaking, there is no single justice, but different species of justice for different domains of action, and someone might be just in one but not in another. For example, someone might be just with respect to keeping promises, but lack justice when it comes to sharing one's abundance with those in need. Likewise, there are different species of temperance, and one person might have some of them but lack others. A person who is moderate when it comes to eating might be immoderate about drinking alcohol, for example. Again, there is no single courage, and having courage in one domain, confronting bullies, let's say, does not entail having courage when it comes to facing painful medical procedures.

Despite this teaching on the disunity of individual virtues, Scotus does think that each species falling under a single genus of virtues, e.g. all the species of prudence, are sufficiently unified that having what Scotus calls "perfect prudence" would entail that one has *all* the species of prudence. This perfect prudence would be "supremely perfect knowledge concerning everything in the domain of possible action, under every condition." Surely only Jesus Christ himself of all human beings has ever had perfect prudence! Similar things may be said for temperance, courage, and justice. This is important because the various species of a single virtue are not related to each other in quite the same way the various species of an animal kind are related to each other. Being a perfect canine does not entail that an animal has all the essential characteristics of every species of canine (dog, wolf, coyote, jackal, etc.), and anyway there couldn't be such a thing. By contrast, perfect justice does entail every species of justice, perfect temperance every species of temperance, and so on. This peculiar way in which species of a single virtue genus are related to each other suggests a deeper sort of unity within each virtue genus than Scotus's comments about the divisibility of each virtue would at first suggest.

THE THEOLOGICAL VIRTUES

There is something sadly ironic about Coleridge's Mariner's famous groan that there is "water, water everywhere nor any drop to drink." He was dying of thirst on the salted sea. But Scotus would say that the plight of thirsty souls bereft of God is sadder still: they are dying of thirst surrounded by fresh water they do not know is there. This is a paradox of the Christian faith, that when we receive it we receive it as living water satisfying a profound thirst, but before receiving we do not recognize it as the water we need. Our hearts may indeed be restless, our souls longing for some unknown God. But all on our own we can fathom neither what glories God intends for human beings, nor the Inner Life of the God who means to glorify us, nor the means by which God intends to glorify us. In short, thirsty as we may be for water beyond the world's end, we do not on our own know how to search for that water or what it would be like if we found it.

The necessity of Revelation is a conditional necessity, conditional on God having greater things in mind for us than we could predict through analysis of our natural capacities. Had He meant no more for us than to live as free beasts, from dust to dust returning, then it would have been sufficient for us to discern of God merely what natural philosophy or metaphysics or morality can show us. But God's topsy-turvy liberality elects to make our dry bones live eternally joyful as resurrected animals, and his chosen means for this supernatural end include disclosure of his trinitarian nature, revelation of himself through the God-Man, Jesus Christ, and the Holy Spirit's establishment of a Church with authority to draw all the nations of the earth closer to God through its sacraments and teaching. The central doctrines of the Christian faith are so fantastical, how can we believe them? How can we hope for ourselves that what they claim is in store for us? How can we make this Triune God the object of our greatest love?

Scotus's answer is the same as the Church's, which is that God himself infuses in us the theological virtues we need in order to believe in, and to will rightly about, those divine things which have been revealed and which could not have been discovered by unaided natural reason. That we depend on God for these virtues is simply a ramification of the orthodox view that we cannot save ourselves. At the same time, and equally importantly, this dependence does not imply fideism, or any sort of view which places theological claims outside the scope of rational investigation. To see this, one need only consider Scotus's intense and tireless arguments, discussed near the outset of this book, for the existence of a First Principle of all things. And from this we could infer how this God might plausibly have made us in part for relationship with himself and, if so, would provide the means for achieving that relationship. So philosophical speculation can, by Scotus's lights, get us very far indeed. But it cannot make us blessed with God in heaven, it cannot yield the specific form that blessedness will take, and it cannot yield God's freely chosen means of getting us there. All this is up to God. To presume we could discover everything on our own, in the rationalistic spirit of a Spinoza or Leibniz, is to denigrate God by denying Him freedom to decide his plans for us.

WHAT'S THE POINT OF THE CARDINAL VIRTUES?

There is something jarring about the theological virtues. They raise at least two conceptual difficulties. The first difficulty is that it seems obvious to us that people who have nothing obviously to do with Christianity can live lives characterized by faith, hope, and love. After all, we talk about "people of faith," an inclusive phrase meant to group all religious believers together, whatever their religious beliefs. And even the philosopher Philippa Foot, who so far as I know had no interest in God, said in her book *Natural Goodness* that we should at least hope that hope will be among the gifts the fairy godmothers bestow on our children in the nursery. As for love, of course we all recognize "mixed motives" even in our best actions, but it strikes us as severe to deny that non-religious people can act in a disinterested way for the good of others. The second difficulty with the doctrine of the infused theological virtues is that they seem to break in on an otherwise fine if humdrum human nature, steering the human animal away from natural ends toward a supernatural end you could never predict just by observing human psychology. Relatedly, it would seem to follow that if God has given you the theological virtues, they're all you need: after all, no amount of success in achieving the merely natural virtues will earn you heaven. So it is worth asking what the point of these natural virtues is, in light of our supernatural end.

In response to the first difficulty, Scotus and other medieval moralists recognized acquired analogues to the theological virtues: acquired faith, or hope, or love. The exact relationship of these to their infused counterparts is a tricky issue which need not detain us. But for any acquired version of a theological virtue, we need to be clear: these are virtues because they help connect us to what is real and do what is really good. Consider acquired faith: credulity as such is not a virtue. Believing falsehoods, even beautiful falsehoods, is not good. So whatever acquired faith is, it is only present when it is helping a person think and act well. Scotus's own example of acquired faith is a person who is learning about the Christian faith and is coming to believe that its doctrines are true, but who hasn't yet been received into the Church. What makes this sort of habit of belief a close cousin of theological faith is precisely in what it inclines the person toward: the truth. For the same reason, Christians are welcome to hold that many non-Christians can have acquired faith insofar as their beliefs about divine things are getting at some truth about divine things, even if it is not the whole truth. The point is well illustrated toward the end of C. S. Lewis's apocalyptic *The Last Battle*, in which the Calormen soldier Emeth has finally seen that Aslan is the true God, and that all his life he has been worshiping a mere idol, Tash, as though Tash were the true God. Emeth is dismayed. But Aslan loves him, telling him, "Child, all the service thou has done to Tash, I account as service to me.... Unless thy desire had been for me thou wouldst not have sought so long and so truly. For all find what they truly seek."

Having nothing to add to those justly famous lines from the master chronicler of Narnia, I'll simply move on to respond to the second difficulty. First, with or without this supernatural end, the cardinal virtues are and remain virtues which perfect our natural powers of intellect and will. There's nothing that even God could do to make it the case, for example, that courage isn't after all the perfection of the irascible appetite. Given human nature, what counts as a virtue of human nature simply follows. And if something is worth existing then it is worth perfecting. Like beauty, goodness is an end in itself. Just as there is no good answer to why we should want to be beautiful, or why we should want to make beautiful things, so too there is no good answer to why we should want to develop habits which make us good. And as far as we can gather, God is not interested in conquering or overwriting our human nature, but in perfecting and glorifying it.

And this brings us to a second response to the second difficulty: the cardinal virtues are not strictly necessary.

God could whisk you to heaven without them. But Scotus's medieval outlook on God and creation and what some theologians call the "economy of salvation" is that God is in the business of abundance. God does not want bare necessities; He does not seem to prefer minimalism. The standing order is that He wants us fully human, and that means perfected by the virtues, even the natural, acquired virtues. It is hard, yes, harder even than yoga or CrossFit. In this light, St. Francis's self-denying spiritual antics make a little more sense. If there was excess it was excess of the sort that is prophetic rather than showy. We cannot make sense of it in the sense that we can see it as something we must do; but we can see it as something that exhorts us to do better than we do. A vain bachelor might train his body to preserve his health and attract the ladies. But this celibate friar trained body and soul in order to be a knight to his Lord and jester to his Lady, of both of whom more anon.

■ 10

FOR JESUS, THROUGH MARY

> [St. Francis] did not stand on his head *in order* to see flowers and trees as a clearer or quainter vision.... Our Lady's Tumbler stood on his head to please Our Lady.... [H]e would go on being a fool; he would become more and more of a fool; he would be the court fool of the King of Paradise.
>
> —G. K. Chesterton, *St. Francis of Assisi*

> Nor were [Christians] likely to determine the place of the Blessed Mary in our reverence, before they had duly secured, in the affections of the faithful, the supreme glory and worship of God Incarnate, her Eternal Lord and Son.
>
> —St. John Henry Newman, *An Essay on the Development of Christian Doctrine*

A WORLD GOOD ENOUGH FOR JESUS

That historical man Jesus Christ said and did things which made even the centurion recognize that he was the Son of God. Divinely inspired reflection on this life produced the testaments to his divinity contained in the New Testament, and those of us born late in time behold that historical person in the light of that revelation: God Incarnate. Few of God's wonders have inspired as much theological reflection as this sublime fact. Like little kids, the theologians have eagerly wondered, "Why?" Why would God do such a marvelous thing as unite himself with our humanity in the most intimate possible way? Bl. John's own answer is astonishing: God's main reason for the Incarnation was simply to be united with the human nature of Jesus Christ. Yes, through his Incarnation and his life, death, and resurrection, He performed the saving work Christianity attributes to Christ. But even if there had been no sin at all and no need of salvation, Christ would have become incarnate anyway. It is a bold argument, but it is not presumptuous. This analysis of divine psychology rests on a firm, foundational teaching of both Scripture and natural theology: that God acts first and foremost for his own good and secondarily for our own good. And what God wanted, for himself, was to become Incarnate in Christ. It is God's party, and we are just guests.

Scotus's view is rather startling given the mainstream understanding of the main purpose of the Incarnation. This understanding makes atonement the main purpose of the Incarnation, where the extraordinary sort of atonement the sons and daughters of Adam and Eve required is supposed to supply the reason for God becoming Man. Some Patristic authors, including Origen and St. Gregory of Nyssa, thought of atonement as God's ransom of the human race, offering himself up to death on the condition that Satan would release his claim of ownership over us sinners. Anselm offered a different view, speculating that human sin had dishonored God. Only a human ought to restore that honor, because the dishonor was due to humans. But only God could restore that honor, so great is the dishonor of sin. For the sake of his honor, therefore, God did the only thing that could be done: he became a man, and as the God-Man fulfilled the twin conditions that man *ought* to do it, and only God *could* do it. John Calvin imagined the human race deserving unspeakable torment, as just punishment for their rebellion. God, loving his elect, willed to undertake that punishment instead. But he could only endure punishment as a man. Therefore, God became man to endure that punishment in our stead. What these theories have in common is that they offer a reason God became man, and different as these theories are they all offer this reason: God became a man in order to fix the problem of human sin. If there weren't that particular problem, then there wouldn't have been Incarnation. And this is why Augustine said that Adam's sin was the *felix culpa*, the happy fault which brought about the Incarnation, the best thing that has ever happened in the history of the universe.

The theology of the *felix culpa* intentionally embraces a head-spinning paradox. The Incarnation is not just the best thing that has happened. By it the universe attains a height of goodness infinitely outstripping whatever goodness it might have had without Incarnation. Yet this goodness is made possible by the first and in one important sense the only true tragedy that has ever befallen the universe. It seems strange, to speak in understatement, that God would endow this world with the crowning jewel of the Incarnation only on condition that its human stewards made a dung-heap of the world.

Duns Scotus solved the paradox by dissolving it. Even if Adam had not sinned, God would have become incarnate anyway. Yes, the Incarnation is the freely chosen means through which God merits for us what we could never merit for ourselves: remission of sin and beatitude in heaven. But God purposed to undertake this saving mission after He had already determined to be united with a human nature. The *culpa* of Adam is still *felix*, but not exactly because it brought about the Incarnation. Instead, it is *felix* because it brought about the atonement: the suffering and death, the burial and resurrection, by which we are saved, and by which we perceive God's extraordinary love. We can have no notion of the tale God can tell himself about the adventures on earth He would have had had Adam never sinned, or had He not bothered about saving Adam's race. But the tale God has told us in the life, death, and resurrection of Christ is the archetype of all our greatest tales: the humble hero whose power is manifest in suffering, and whose suffering lifts up the downtrodden and sets the captives free. The loremaster Tolkien, in his essay "On Fairy Stories," recognized that the Gospel is the greatest tale, the one that happens to be true, but is also the best.

As a scholar and a priest, and as a mendicant friar who would have walked on foot from Scotland to Oxford, from Oxford to whatever port would bear him to the shores of France, and from Paris to Cologne, Scotus lived his part in the great sequel to that tale, the sequel which tells of the Church's efforts to evangelize the world. As a scholar he pursued the *quaestio*, the intellectual question which is also a quest. As a priest, at Mass he continually re-enacted the best part of the original tale, the Triduum; and in the confessional he counseled sinners and spoke the words of absolution they needed to hear in order to live up to their parts in the drama of creation. Living his life in and as a tale, he had no need to write as a storyteller. His writing was for other purposes. And when it came to the purpose of the Incarnation he did not tell the tale of the Gospel prettily, for he was focused on more fundamental things.

When it came to putting down in writing the purpose of the Incarnation, Scotus focused on the main thing which itself does not make much of a tale but enables all tales. He focused on God's inner life, and in particular on God's love of himself. God is the most orderly lover. He loves creatures extravagantly, but not because He withholds from himself the supreme love which He deserves. God loves himself most of all, and even loves all other things for his own sake. It is not fair to blame Him for being selfish; it would be unseemly for God to be otherwise, even if He could be, and this is because God is the Good itself. Sometimes human authors talk about the *need* to write. They are exaggerating. No author needs to write. If there is need there is no real authorship. And so it is with God. God freely chooses to compose the tale of creation, and He does it because He wants to, because it pleases his majesty. This is the wellspring of all creation: it pleases his majesty.

Now imagine God thinking of the tales He could tell. He conceives in his mind the human nature of Christ, in some sense as C. S. Lewis conceived in his mind the picture of a faun with an umbrella, carrying a stack of parcels under a lampstand in a snowy forest. The picture was beautiful, so Lewis decided to write a story in which that picture would take on the sort of reality it could have in a story. Likewise, God sees the human nature of Christ, and decides to write a story in which He really lives in the world united with that nature as one person, one person enjoying the divine and human natures. That is the picture which inspires the story. Having decided to write a story, God determines to make the God-Man the protagonist, organizing every detail around him, as Lewis organized the details of Cair Paravel and the Pevensie children, the White Witch and her Turkish Delight, and the Beavers and Father Christmas, around that picture of the faun. We do not fault him for not organizing the story around the Lion, Aslan, because Lewis is a man, and that usually means starting with images—of fauns, say—and working up through the images to the Main Thing.

All the details of what God did with his world-unifying picture of the Incarnate Lord are a tale better told elsewhere. But the part that has to do with what Scotus had to say picks up where we left off, at the remedy for that fault of Adam which Augustine called happy. Even in the tale as Scotus perceived it, it is a happy fault, but not for the reason Augustine thought. The Fall did not force God's hand to become man. But it was even happier than Augustine imagined. Emmanuel, God is with us, not because we're miserable but simply because we exist. When it comes down to it, God simply wanted a world in which you and I would be invited to become subjects of its lawful King, regardless of the stain of our sins. Because He wanted us in the realm despite our sin, his desire for union took on the character of a mission of redemption. But the mission is not the main thing. Union with God, in Christ, is the main thing, at least insofar as the main thing concerns us. And therefore it is fitting that God began that mission as a baby, whereby we have union with Christ through his mother. He began his human life in that intimate union with creation which we call *in utero*: in the womb of the greatest saint of the Church, the Blessed Virgin Mary.

A MOTHER GOOD ENOUGH FOR JESUS

As we approach the end of this book about Scotus it is good to remember the beginning, in which we saw that Scotus thinks of God as the First Final Cause, the ultimate purpose of everything in the universe. In some sense, even if it's a distant sense, everything happens for God's sake, even—in a way often opaque to us—the bad things. The ultimate and best answer to why God made this world at all is this: He made it for himself. But the next-best answer to that question is this: He made it for Jesus. He crafted a world-story in which the God-Man would be the main character, experiencing the greatest range of what is possible for creatures to experience: the greatest agony and the greatest joy, the profoundest shame and the highest honor. The story of the world has no red herrings and no loose ends; the plot is water-tight and there are no accidents. All is ordered by love.

It was in contemplation of this story and its central character that Scotus alighted upon the argument which was to become his most highly-valued intellectual contribution to the Church. It is his teaching on the Immaculate Conception of the Blessed Virgin Mary, and in particular the manner in which he argued for the doctrine, which has given Scotus an unending place of prominence. Indeed, the doctrine is dogma, having been solemnly promulgated in 1854 by Pope Pius IX. And do not forget that Pope St. John Paul II, not long after Scotus's beatification, praised him as a theological warrior-poet, the Defender of the

Immaculate Conception and the Minstrel of the Incarnation. This is, by the way, a fitting pairing of titles, about which we will say more shortly.

For now, let us bring to our mind the dogma itself. For all the controversy it sparked in the Middle Ages, and for all the division it causes between Protestants and Catholics today, the full statement of the dogma is disarmingly brief: "the most Blessed Virgin Mary, in the first instance of her conception, by a singular grace and privilege granted by Almighty God, in view of the merits of Jesus Christ, the Savior of the human race, was preserved free from all stain of original sin." That is it.

The theological difficulty with embracing this view arises when we consider St. Augustine's influential understanding of original sin, according to which it is a condition of corruption literally *inherited* from Adam and Eve, father and mother to son and daughter, down the long years. On one almost equally influential understanding of the main purpose of the Incarnation—but, as we have seen, not on Scotus's—God became man to save us from this corruption and the guilt we incur as a result of it. At first glance, therefore, to exempt Mary from the stain of original sin is to imply either that she is not really a daughter of Eve—and no one ever thought that (in spite of strange speculations about the manner in which her parents, Sts. Joachim and Anna, conceived her)—or that she is not in need of Christ's aid for her salvation, or both. And even if we note that the dogmatic formula affirms that it is in view of the *merits of Christ* that Mary was preserved from original sin, and not her own merits, we're left to wonder what exactly it is about Christ's merits of which Mary stands in need, if Christ's merits were accrued precisely for the purpose of cleansing or saving or redeeming human beings.

And here is where we must come back to John Paul II's felicitous pairing of titles: Defender of the Immaculate

Conception and Minstrel of the Incarnation. For it is in the light of Christ that Our Lady shines most brightly. When we contemplate the cosmic centrality of Christ—not just his centrality in the story of our salvation, but centrality in the story of the very existence of the world—then the great honor due to the Blessed Virgin Mary simply makes sense. What God wanted in creation is for Jesus to exist, and everything else to exist for Jesus. Jesus is the King of the Cosmos, and cannot be worshiped excessively, because he is the Highest Good. But God chose Mary, of all women, to be the Mother of Jesus. Before all time, in what we might think of as the stage of creation in which God is dreaming it all up, God knew Mary. But he also knew every other possible woman. Yet she was selected to be the Mother of Jesus. It is an inconceivably lofty honor, to be so close to Christ. Her blood in his veins; his blood in hers. To have such high rank in the realm and court of Christ the King—literally, the Queen Mother! Sheer awe at the marvel of a woman raised above angels should prompt us to apply superlatives to her. And the pious logic by which Scotus defended the superlative of the Immaculate Conception is that the degree and type of honors we give to Mary should be checked only by the *prohibition* of Scripture and the Church. Where the Bible and the Church do not forbid giving some honor to Mary, we should give it to her.

Mothering God is an honor no human being, however great, can deserve. Only someone who didn't understand, or had forgotten, what God is could think that *if only* Mary were without original sin, then that would be sufficient to make her *deserve* to be the Mother of God. Of course she doesn't! With or without original sin, neither she nor anyone else is entitled, off her own bat, however clean, to that honor. Scotus reminds us, over and over again, that no facts about creatures or possible creatures *compel* God to do anything: it is all bounty with Him. So when

God knew Mary before she was born, what did He see in her? Did He see her stained by original sin but then resolve to bring her into the world free from that stain, cleansing her before she even existed? Or did He always see her free from the stain, never in need of cleansing? In neither case could God be compelled to make her the Mother of Jesus; remember, it's all bounty. But one of these options gives Mary the greater honor, and thus, for Scotus anyway, the answer is clear: there was never a moment in which God knew Mary as guilty of sin.

The order of God's love is not the same as the order of time. Mary's eternal preservation from original sin is itself the *result* of a definite event which took place just outside Jerusalem two thousand years ago. On the cross, Christ merited not just remission of sins for all sinners, and not just the beatification in heaven of all human beings. His merits far outstrip these, for his merits are infinite. To what additional mediations might these infinite merits then be applied? Theological imagination should err, if at all, on the side of abundance. And Bl. John's theological imagination identified one additional, logically possible, way in which Christ's merits could be enjoyed by a human being, namely this: they could preserve someone from ever being stained by sin. God could save someone in this way; it is fitting that He would save someone in this way, as a testament to the full scope of Christ's infinite merits; it is also fitting that, should He choose to save just one person in this preemptive way, it would be Mary. It is fitting to pick Mary for this honor not because He was afraid He'd get dirty if He were born of a less clean woman, but because it was a decent and generous way to honor His Mother, and a magnanimous way to arrange for his own dwelling place among us. So, God could do it, it was fitting for Him to do it; therefore, Scotus and the Church reason, God did do it. In the Latin summary: *potuit, decuit, ergo fecit*; God was able, it was fitting, therefore God did it.

As a form of theological reasoning there is something in this four-word argument which defies the rationalistic spirit, both in philosophy and theology. Clearly the argument is not deductive; the conclusion is not entailed by the premises. And when it comes to God and the fact that his ways are so often hidden from us, getting to *fecit* simply from *potuit* and *decuit* seems to be a solid case of reasoning ahead of one's data. Oddly, however, it is an argument at home in the mind of a man who had written so compellingly and frequently about God's love, freedom, and abundant generosity that he practically came to expect extravagance from God. As a logician and metaphysician, Scotus would have known that his famous argument falls rather short of the apodictic ideal he sought in so many other aspects of his thought. But in this case, he was convicted by the logic of filial affection. A child might become so confident in the love and generosity of her father that she forms reasonable expectations about what he will do: of course he will give me a big hug when I get hurt; of course he will buy me a present on my birthday. In making these judgments about her father she is not reasoning deductively, but we would be not only rather nasty but actually mistaken to think that in the absence of deductive certainty about the forthcoming hug and present, she should lower her degree of confidence that the hug and present really are forthcoming. She can have all the confidence in the world her father will do these things, without any presumption and without any disrespectful limitation of her father's freedom. She knows her father, loves her father, and is confident of his love for her. Therefore her confidence is rational. So, too, Scotus's confidence in God's uniquely great gift of Christ's merits to Mary is not a rationalistic confidence, but it is very rational, because it rests on those reasons which come from love.

Dignare me Laudare te Virgo sacrata

APPENDIX

SOURCES AND FURTHER READINGS

APPROACHING SCOTUS

There is much, much more to learn about Blessed John, on both the topics I have treated here and those topics I have not treated at all. Readers of this book who already knew a lot about Scotus may wonder why I did not also cover other topics, or why I focused on just the topics I did. My answer to them is that I have spent most of my adult life as a Scotus scholar, and these are the topics which (i) interest me most and (ii) really do seem to me to be central to Scotus's way of looking at God and the world. Around the seminar table I would, of course, be willing to revise my judgments in light of good reasons to the contrary. But another important answer is that the topics I have discussed here, limited as they are, are the ones which I also judged to be of most intrinsic interest to readers encountering Scotus for the first time. It is for those of you who didn't already know Scotus well that I have written this book, and I hope what you have read here has been edifying and has helped you to learn *about*, and maybe even *from*, this complicated and blessed friar. In case, in the course of reading through this book, you have developed a desire to learn more, I have curated a list of further readings which will suffice for a lifetime of study.

In addition to his *Quodlibetal Questions* and *Ordinatio*, Scotus wrote two *Sentences* commentaries, the *Lectura* and the *Reportationes*; some commentaries on Aristotle; and two short works, *Theoremata* and *On the First Principle* (*De Primo Principio*). He wrote in Latin, and most of what he wrote is now available in modern, printed editions which have been carefully edited by scholars. Quite a lot has been translated into English, much of it due to the generous work of the greatest English-speaking Scotus scholar of the twentieth century, Fr. Allan B. Wolter, OFM.

There are two important and easily accessible English Scotus anthologies worth noting: *Duns Scotus: Philosophical Writings*, translated by Allan Wolter (Indianapolis: Hackett Publishing Co., 1987); and *John Duns Scotus: Selected Writings on Ethics*, translated by Thomas Williams (Oxford: Oxford University Press, 2017), which more or less supersedes Wolter's anthology *Duns Scotus on the Will and Morality* (Washington, D.C.: Catholic University of America Press, 1997)—though Wolter's introduction to this anthology is still very valuable.

Allan Wolter and Felix Alluntis translated the *Quodlibetal Questions* and published them as *God and Creatures* (Princeton: Princeton University Press, 1975). Wolter also translated *On the First Principle*, publishing it as *A Treatise on God as First Principle* (Chicago: Franciscan Herald Press, 1966), the revised 1982 edition of which contains an extensive commentary on this notoriously difficult work. As for *Ordinatio* and the other *Sentences* commentaries, there is no complete English version of it or them. But bits and pieces, on a wide range of topics, have been published in many scattered volumes. Of special note here are the translations of Books I and IV of a version of Scotus's *Reportationes.* Book I was translated in two volumes by Allan Wolter and Oleg Bychkov (St. Bonaventure, NY: Franciscan Institute Publications, 2008), and Bychkov and Trent Pomplun published Book IV in two volumes a few years later (St. Bonaventure, NY: Franciscan Institute Publications, 2016). In recent years the philosopher Peter Simpson has been publishing his translations of Scotus's *Ordinatio* on his website: www.aristotelophile.com/current.htm. An indispensable resource for both the scholar and the layperson is the bibliography produced by Tobias Hoffman. Among other features, it has a section devoted to English translations of Scotus's works, which includes over fifty entries in the latest edition. The "Duns Scotus Bibliography from 1950 to the Present" may be found at https://www.academia.edu/84553496/Duns_Scotus_Bibliography_from_1950_to_the_Present_10th_edition_August_2022_. Turning now from Scotus's own writing to writing about Scotus, the best short introduction to Scotus's life is Allan B. Wolter's "Reflections on the Life and Works of Scotus," in *Scotus and Ockham: Selected Essays* (St. Bonaventure, NY: Franciscan Institute Publications, 2003). A good and even shorter biography may be found in the introductory essay in Thomas Williams's *The Cambridge Companion to Duns Scotus* (Cambridge: Cambridge University Press, 2003). Antonie Vos's trilogy on Scotus contains about as much documentable biographical material as we have—but remember, that still isn't much: *The Philosophy of John Duns Scotus* (Edinburgh: Edinburgh University Press, 2006), *The Theology of John Duns Scotus* (Leiden: Brill, 2018), *John Duns Scotus: A Life* (Kampen: Summum Academic, 2018). For hagiography, Fr. Stefano Manelli's *Blessed John Duns Scotus: Marian Doctor* (New Bedford, MA: Academy of the Immaculate, 2011) is a heartwarming read.

The best introductions to Scotus's thought in English are Richard Cross, *Duns Scotus* (Oxford: Oxford University Press, 1999); Antonie Vos, *The Philosophy of John Duns Scotus* and *The Theology of John Duns Scotus*; Sr. Mary Beth Ingham, *Understanding John Duns Scotus: Of Realty the Rarest-veined Unraveller* (St. Bonaventure, NY: Franciscan Institute Publications, 2017); Sr. Mary Beth Ingham and Mechthild Dreyer, *The Philosophical Vision of John Duns Scotus: An Introduction* (Washington, D.C.: Catholic University of America Press, 2004); and Etienne Gilson, *John Duns Scotus: Introduction to His Fundamental Positions*, trans. James G. Colbert (Edinburgh: T&T Clark, 2019). Of these, I especially recommend Sr. Mary Beth's *Understanding John Duns Scotus* if you would like to read at least one more book on Scotus and you do not already have philosophical training.

On the history of Scotism, Colman J. Majchrzak's *A Brief History of Bonaventurianism* (Washington, D.C.: Catholic University of America Press, 1957) makes it clear that, from about 1500 to 1920, Scotus was officially recognized by Franciscans themselves as the most important Franciscan theologian. I think the best single source on the history of Scotism is Trent Pomplun, "John Duns Scotus in the History of Medieval Philosophy from the Sixteenth Century to Étienne Gilson (†1978)" (*Bulletin de philosophie médiévale* 58, 2016). Pomplun has also written the best thing I know of on the history of Gerard Manley Hopkins's interest in John Duns Scotus: "The Theology of Gerard Manley Hopkins: From John Duns Scotus to the Baroque" (*The Journal of Religion* 95, 2015).

THE EXISTENCE OF GOD

Scotus's arguments for God's existence are found in his treatise *De Primo Principio* and in the *Ordinatio*. Both versions of the arguments have, thankfully, been translated: *De Primo Principio* in Wolter's *A Treatise on God as First Principle*, and the *Ordinatio* texts in Wolter's *Duns Scotus: Philosophical Writings*. Richard Cross wrote an extremely helpful analysis and evaluation of Scotus's arguments in *Duns Scotus on God* (Aldershot: Ashgate, 2005). The metaphysician Timothy O'Connor has published two rigorous analyses on aspects of Scotus's arguments: "Scotus on the Existence of a First Efficient Cause" (*International Journal for Philosophy of Religion* vol. 33, 1993) and "From First Efficient Cause to God: Scotus on the Identification Stage of the Cosmological Argument," in *John Duns Scotus: Metaphysics & Ethics* (Leiden: Brill, 1996), edited by Ludger Honnefelder and others. Both of O'Connor's essays are available at his website, www.toconnor.org. Valuable as these studies from Cross and O'Connor are, in my judgment Scotus's arguments have yet to receive the full justice they deserve from contemporary philosophers of religion. Maybe the bare sketches I was able to offer in this book will inspire some of you to mine the full depths of these arguments and bring out all their treasures for our instruction and delight.

For some of the relevant Franciscan background, I recommend A. G. Little, *The Grey Friars in Oxford* (Oxford: Oxford University Press, 1892), and John Moorman, *A History of the Franciscan Order from Its Origins to the Year 1517* (Oxford: Oxford University Press, 1968). I have also consulted Moorman's *Medieval Franciscan Houses* (St. Bonaventure, NY: Franciscan Institute Publications, 1983); David Knowles and R. Neville Hadcock, *Medieval Religious Houses: England and Wales* (New York: St. Martin's, 1971); Knowles's *The Religious Orders in England*, vol. 1 (Cambridge: Cambridge University Press, 1948); and Little's *Franciscan Papers, Lists, and Documents* (Manchester: Manchester University Press, 1943).

SPEAKING OF GOD

The most important primary text for Scotus's doctrine of univocity is *Ordinatio* I.3, and the relevant sections are in Wolter's *Duns Scotus: Philosophical Writings*. The text from Aquinas on which

I based my reconciling interpretation of Scotus and Aquinas is *Summa theologiae* I.13.5, which is widely available, including at www.newadvent.org/summa/. The best scholarly resources for understanding Duns Scotus's doctrine of univocity are Richard Cross, "Where Angels Fear to Tread," *Antonianum* 76 (2001): 7-41; and Thomas Williams, "The Doctrine of Univocity Is True and Salutary," *Modern Theology* 21 (2005): 575–85. A recent book from Daniel P. Horan, OFM, *Postmodernity and Univocity* (Minneapolis: Fortress Press, 2014), offers a nice exposition of the way in which Scotus has been abused, and his doctrine of univocity misunderstood, by some influential modern theologians and intellectual historians.

William de la Mare's *Correction* may be found in English translation at Prof. Simpson's website: https://www.aristotelophile.com/current.htm. Pope St. Pius X's 1914 motu proprio *Doctoris Angelici* may be read at https://maritain.nd.edu/jmc/etext/doctoris.htm, and the supplemental Twenty-Four Propositions at https://franciscan-archive.org/thomas/24theses.html.

Readers might also be interested to know that Pius X's instructions to make Aquinas the foundation of philosophical education were more or less enshrined in the 1917 revision to the Code of Canon Law (see canons 589.1 and 1366.2) and remained in the 1983 revision (see canon 252.3), which is the currently authoritative edition. Finally, in this chapter I mentioned Peter Lombard's *Sentences*. This work is translated in four volumes by Giulio Silano (Toronto: Pontifical Institute for Medieval Studies, 2007-2010).

THE BIGGEST BIG QUESTION

In my studies of Scotus I have benefited enormously from reading, and reading about, St. Francis, and I tried to impart some of that benefit to you through this book. For the Francis material, I recommend *The Complete St. Francis: His Life, The Complete Writings, and the Little Flowers*, translated and edited, with an introduction, by Jon M. Sweeney (Orleans, MA: Paraclete Press, 2015). This volume also contains the classic Sabatier biography of St. Francis. A very different sort of biography is G. K. Chesterton's *St. Francis of Assisi*; Chesterton has the ability to make anything sound interesting, and when he writes about something which is already extremely interesting, like St. Francis, he is incandescent. In the same vein, Chesterton's Aquinas biography, *The Dumb Ox*, deserves seriously joyful attention. It is a minor tragedy that Chesterton never wrote a companion piece on Scotus. He might have called it *The Tonsured Eagle*.

The issues under consideration in this chapter are drawn from several places in Scotus's works, but the most important texts include *Reportatio* I.36, to be found in the second volume of the Wolter and Bychkov translation of *Reportatio* I; and various texts in Williams's *John Duns Scotus: Selected Ethical Writings*, especially *Ordinatio* I.38 and I.44. Timothy Noone has written two magisterial studies on Duns Scotus's understanding of the Divine Ideas: "Scotus on Divine Ideas" (*Medioevo* 24, 1998) and "Aquinas on Divine Ideas: Scotus's Evaluation" (*Franciscan Studies* 56, 1998). For exposition of Aquinas's views on these matters, Gregory T. Doolan's *Aquinas on the Divine Ideas as Exemplar Causes* (Washington, D.C.: Catholic University of America, 2008) is a readable and reliable guide. I have made a contribution of my own in Ward, *Divine Ideas* (Cambridge: Cambridge University Press, 2020), in which I try to defend a broadly Scotistic view against a variety of competing alternatives.

THE CREATED ORDER

The most important primary texts for Scotus's distinctive version of hylomorphism are *Lectura* II.12 (not translated, as far as I know), and *Questions on the* Metaphysics *of Aristotle* VII.20, which was translated along with the whole of the *Questions on the* Metaphysics *of Aristotle* by Girard Etzkorn and Allan Wolter, and published in two volumes (St. Bonaventure, NY: Franciscan Institute Publications, 1998). Here too I have tried to make a contribution, in Ward, *John Duns Scotus on Parts, Wholes, and Hylomorphism* (Leiden: Brill, 2014). Richard Cross's *The Physics of Duns Scotus* (Oxford: Oxford University Press, 1998) is a brilliant and relevant source. For Scotus's realism about common natures, see *Ordinatio* II.3, translated in *Five Texts on the Mediaeval Problem of Universals*, translated and edited by Paul Vincent Spade (Indianapolis, IN: Hackett Publishing Company, 1994). A challenging but trusty secondary source is Peter King's "Duns Scotus on the Common Nature" (*Philosophical Topics* 20, 1992).

YOU ARE UNIQUE

Scotus worked out his theory of what makes individuals unique in the same context as his theory of realism. Therefore Spade's *Five Texts* is the place to go. Allan Wolter has a helpful essay on Scotus in *Individuation in Scholasticism: The Later Middle Ages and the Counter-Reformation, 1150–1650*, edited by Jorge J. E. Gracia (Albany, NY: SUNY Press, 1994).

PURPOSES NATURAL AND DIVINE

For Scotus on what is self-evident to us, including those aspects of our own thinking which are self-evident to us, see the sections on knowledge in Wolter's *Philosophical Writings* anthology. The two most important primary texts for understanding Scotus on purposes and final causes are *De Primo Principio* II (translated by Wolter) and *Questions on the* Metaphysics *of Aristotle* V.1 (translated by Etzkorn and Wolter). The most helpful secondary source I have found is Marilyn McCord Adams, "Final Causality and Explanation in Scotus's *De Primo Principio*," in *Nature in Medieval Thought*, ed. Chumaru Koyama (Leiden: Brill, 2000). The quotation from *Dream of the Rood* is taken from Charles W. Kennedy's translation (In parentheses Publications, 2000).

TWO AFFECTIONS OF THE WILL

The Anselmian background to Scotus's theory of the will may be found in Anselm's *On Freedom of Choice*, *On the Fall of the Devil*, and *De Concordia*, all translated by Thomas Williams in *Anselm: Basic Writings* (Indianapolis, IN: Hackett Publishing Company, 2007). Scotus discusses Anselm's theory at least three times, once in each *Sentences* commentary (*Lectura*, *Ordinatio*, *Reportationes*), at II.6. The *Ordinatio* discussion may be found in Williams's *Selected Writings on Ethics*. Peter King has argued that Duns Scotus is not so very Anselmian after all. As always, King's argument is worth reading carefully and taking seriously; see King, "Scotus's Rejection of Anselm: The Two-Wills Theory," published in the *Proceedings of the Quadruple Scotus Congress* (St. Bonaventure, NY: Franciscan Institute Publications, 2010), and also at his website: http://individual.utoronto.ca/pking/. In the end I disagree with Professor King, as my chapter on this topic makes obvious. For helping me think better about Scotus's adoption of Anselm's theory of the will, I am grateful to my former student Seth Howton.

On the relationship between self-love and love for God, Thomas M. Osborne is a good guide; see his *Love of Self and Love of God in Thirteenth-Century Ethics* (Notre Dame, IN: Notre Dame University Press, 2005). Finally, while it is not on Scotus, Robert M. Adams's essay "Pure Love" is the best thing I've ever read on the relationship between self-love and love for God; I wouldn't be surprised to learn that it has had an influence on the way I read Scotus. Adams's essay may be found in his book *The Virtue of Faith* (Oxford: Oxford University Press, 1987).

THE VIRTUOUS LIFE

For Scotus's reflections on the virtues, the most important primary texts in English are to be found in Thomas Williams's *John Duns Scotus: Selected Writings in Ethics.* For background, see Bonnie Kent, *Virtues of the Will: The Transformation of Ethics in the Late Thirteenth Century* (Washington, D.C.: Catholic University of America, 1995). For Scotus on the possibility of acquired versions of theological virtue, see Scott Williams's entry on Scotus in *The Oxford Handbook of the Epistemology of Theology*, edited by William J. Abraham and Frederick D. Aquino (Oxford: Oxford University Press, 2017).

FOR JESUS, THROUGH MARY

The central primary text for Scotus's thinking about the primacy of the Incarnation is *Ordinatio* III.7. Translations of this and other relevant texts may be found in *Franciscan Christology: Selected Texts, Translations, and Introductory Essays*, edited by Damian McElrath (St. Bonaventure, NY: Franciscan Institute Publications, 1980). For Scotus's thinking about the Immaculate Conception, see *Ordinatio* III.3. For translations of relevant texts see *Four Questions on Mary*, translated by Allan B. Wolter (St. Bonaventure, NY: Franciscan Institute Publications, 2012). Marilyn McCord Adams's *Christ and Horrors* (Cambridge: Cambridge University Press, 2006) contains rich material on the background to Scotus's views about the primacy of the

Incarnation, as well as careful analysis of Scotus's reasons for embracing it. An important new book is Justus H. Hunter, *If Adam Had Not Sinned: The Reason for the Incarnation from Anselm to Scotus* (Washington, D.C.: Catholic University of America, 2020). Pastorally and spiritually sensitive studies include Fr. Maximilian Mary Dean, *A Primer on the Absolute Primacy of Christ: Blessed John Duns Scotus and the Franciscan Thesis* (New Bedford, MA: Academy of the Immaculate, 2006) and Fr. Ruggero Rosini, *Mariology of Blessed John Duns Scotus*, translated and published by the Franciscans of the Immaculate (New Bedford, MA: Academy of the Immaculate, 2008). Tolkien's essay, "On Fairy Stories," may be found in J. R. R. Tolkien, *Tales from the Perilous Realm* (Boston: Houghton Mifflin Harcourt, 2008).

Beate Ioannes Duns Scote,
ora pro nobis.

INDEX OF NAMES

ABOUT THE AUTHOR

THOMAS M. WARD, PhD (UCLA), MPhil (Oxon.) is a historian of the philosophy and theology of the Middle Ages. He is the author of *Divine Ideas* and *John Duns Scotus on Parts, Wholes, and Hylomorphism*, and the translator of Duns Scotus's *Treatise on the First Principle* (*De Primo Principio*). Ward is an associate professor of philosophy at Baylor University in Waco, Texas.

Made in the USA
Las Vegas, NV
08 May 2023